Kingdom
Power and Glory

Kingdom Power and Glory

A historical guide to Westminster Abbey

John Field

First published 1996
© John Field 1996
Reprinted 1998
Second edition 1999

Hardback edition ISBN 0 907383 726
Softback edition ISBN 0 907383 718

New photographs © Malcolm Crowthers 1996

Design and photographic direction: Robin Farrow
Design: Melissa Alaverdy and Julia Rheam

Picture research: Ruth King

Printed in Italy by G. Canale & C. S.p.A. - Borgaro T.se - Turin

Published by James & James (Publishers) Limited
Gordon House Business Centre
6 Lissenden Gardens
London NW5 1LX

Picture Acknowledgements

Ashmolean Museum 83; Bayeux 18–9 (top); 19 (bottom); 21; Bridgeman Art Library 114–5; British Library 23 (upper margin); 24 (top); 25 (middle right); 28 (bottom); 51; 76 (top); 84–5; Donald Buttress 110; Tariq Chaudry 48 (lower margin); Chetham's Library Manchester 16 (upper margin); 16 (middle right); 20 (upper margin); CDT Seine-Maritime 16 (lower margin); Corpus Christi College, Cambridge 27 (upper margin); 37 (bottom right); Express Syndication 153; Robin Farrow 8 (top); Jeremy Gower 9 (margin); 13; 17 (upper margin); 24 (upper margin); 25 (right); 35 (upper margin); 38 (middle margin); 39 (top); 47 (lower margin); 56 (middle margin); 116 (middle margin); 134 (middle margin); Hampton Court 97 (lower margin); Hulton Getty Picture Collection 138 (lower margin); 140; 141 (lower margin); 142 (lower margin); 143 (upper margin); Illustrated London News 136 (lower margin); Mansell Collection 121; Mary Evans Picture Library 128 (upper margin); 132 (upper margin); Museum of London 10 (upper margin); 82 (upper margin); 94 (bottom); 130 (lower margin); National Gallery 46; National Portrait Gallery 54 (upper margin); l78 (margin); 78 (lower margin); 91 (upper margin); 95; Rebecca Naden/PA News 152; John Stillwell/PA News 31; Royal Collection Enterprises 123; 133 (top); University Library, Cambridge 10 (bottom); 11 (top); 27 (lower margin); Westminster Abbey Library frontispiece; 11 (bottom); 17 (bottom); 19 (bottom); 26; 29 (bottom); 34; 35; 40; 58 (upper margin); 60 (lower margin); 63; 64; 67 (bottom); 78 (upper margin); 80 (top and bottom); 82 (lower margin); 84 (upper margin); 92 (lower margin); 94 (lower margin); 102; 103 (upper margin); 104 (lower margin); 108 (upper margin); 109 (lower); 110; 116 (lower margin); 117 (lower margin); 118; 120 (top and bottom); 124 (upper margin); 130; 131 (top left and lower margin); 132 (lower margin); 134 (lower margin); 135 (top left and bottom); 136 (upper margin); 139 (lower margin); 141 (upper margin); 144 (lower margin); 146 (bottom); 148 (upper margin); 151 (lower margin); Westminster City Archive 80 (bottom); 103 (lower margin); 108 (bottom); 122; 126 (lower margin); Westminster School Governing Body 87; Joanna Woodmansterne 57 (bottom)

Illustrations

Half-title:	Corbel of an angel bearing the arms of Edward the Confessor, on the north side of Dean's Yard
Frontispiece:	The Abbey Eucharist on St Peter's Day
Title page:	Angel playing a viole, border decoration from the Litlyngton Missal
Foreword:	The Abbey from Dean's Yard
Preface:	Damaged Weeper (mourner) from the tomb of John of Eltham

Foreword
by the Dean of Westminster

The twin towers of Westminster Abbey's West front are famous throughout the world. They have become a symbol not just of London but of Great Britain. They also stand for the presence of the Christian faith at the heart of the capital. For millions of visitors the Abbey is a 'must' on their tourist agenda. Within and around this great building a community today still lives, prays and works together.

The Abbey's history has been often written. But this is not just another history. It is an informative, sometimes idiosyncratic, and always enjoyable account of this remarkable place. It brings the history to life and connects it with the work of Westminster Abbey today. The author interprets the building to those who come as tourists or pilgrims, and invites you to share the spirit of the place that he has captured so well.

John Field understands the complicated life of the Abbey better than most. For thirty years he was a teacher at Westminster School and its Archivist and Librarian. So he has himself lived in this community and therefore knows that the Abbey's life in every generation has been and is based upon the daily worship of God, which continues without fail throughout the year.

On behalf of all at Westminster Abbey, I commend this book. You will learn more about the building. You will hear stories from history, which possibly you did not know. And you will perceive how today's Abbey is maintaining and developing the rich tradition of worship and service in which it stands.

Wesley Carr
The Deanery,
Westminster

Preface

I fell under the spell of the Abbey in 1963, and lived in the precinct under its protection for over 30 years. There I came to know Lawrence Tanner and John Carleton, and, through them, the long- dead Francis Westlake. Theirs is the tradition I have humbly tried to follow. They were storytellers who carried their learning lightly, and relished the detail or anecdote which captured character or period with the force of metaphor.

I am no scholar, and freely admit that my presumptuous approach to history is weighted towards the literary and the imaginative. I have been fortunate to have the patient guidance of those more learned than I. In treading the highroad of English history, about which everyone knows something, I fear that two of my objectives, to found my account upon scrupulous accuracy, and to include nothing which would offend a true scholar, will be snatched away by readers whose knowledge exceeds mine. But my prime purpose is to celebrate the extraordinary diversity of human events to which the Abbey has been witness; in this respect the cast and their lines need no apology.

A work that springs from the heart, as this does, should pay more than usual attention to the head. Head and heart combine in gratitude to all who have generously given encouragement and advice, especially The Dean and Chapter of Westminster, Donald Buttress, Edward and Lilian Carpenter, Pamela Carrington, Barbara Harvey, Iris Hughes, Richard Mortimer, Enid Nixon, Frances Ramsey, Christine Reynolds, Tony Trowles and Brian Young. I am grateful to the many members of the Abbey community who have taken an interest in the project and have been willing to give up their time to talk to me about it.

John Field
May 1996

For all who have loved and served Westminster Abbey

Contents

1.

'Sand-banks, marshes, forests, savages, — precious little to eat fit for a civilized man, nothing but Thames water to drink. . . . death skulking in the air, in the water, . . .'   Joseph Conrad, *Heart of Darkness*

Geography and Legend
Before 1045

Above the narrows where the first bridge will be built, the river edges a mile of hard strand and then broadens into a marshy waste. Here the land is treacherous. There are backwaters of alluvial mud, swampy channels liable to flood. Streams from the uplands to the north thread it as they seek the main artery; ditches try feebly to drain it. The giant ox, the narrow-nosed rhinoceros and the straight-tusked elephant inhabit here. Here and there are little islands of gravel or firmer sand, inhospitable except for those who love or need the fens.

A primitive world lurks in the Abbey: this Green Man, staring through the foliage of his own hair on the 14th century gate of the Chapel of the Pew feels far older than Christianity.

But a wide river is fordable, and islands defended by muddy moats attract the prudent. There may have been scattered settlements before the Romans came in 43 BC, but it is only with the Romans that maps and names begin. Julius Caesar wrote that the Thames was fordable at just one place, but no one now can be certain where that was. Chelsea and Westminster are the nearest claimants to Roman Londinium. A 19th-century Westminster schoolboy's story, before the river was embanked, that at low tide he could walk across the river just upstream of Westminster Bridge, and the water never came higher than his knees, is one kind of evidence for a ford at Westminster; Roman maps suggest another. To the north of the marsh, Watling Street; to the south-east, Dover Street. They peter out in a boggy limbo, but both point at an island stepping-stone, a rough square of gravel about four hundred yards across, forming a delta for one of the main tributary streams from the north. The pragmatic Romans may have settled here, on Thorn Ey — Bramble Island — which looks pivotal for their transport. A reused stone sarcophagus unearthed to the north of the Abbey, and a fragment of roof tile found beneath the Norman Undercroft of the monastic dormitory attest their presence, however flimsily. Conclusive evidence for the site of the ford is deep under Thames mud, or washed away down to the estuary.

So Thorney was chosen. Sister islands up and down stream: Chels-Ey — limestone landing — Bermond's Ey and Batter's-Ey,

9

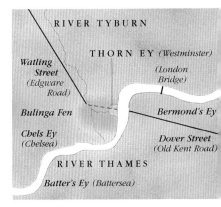

'IN MEMORY OF VALERIUS AMANDINUS MADE BY VALERIUS SUPERVENTOR AND VALERIUS MARCELLUS FOR THEIR FATHER'

Reused Christian Roman sarcophagus found under the North Green (St Margaret's Churchyard) in 1869.

named after later settlers called Beornmund and Beaduric, were temporarily disdained. A thousand years after the Romans arrived Thorney Island was to become the crown and diadem of the kingdom, the site of both the royal palace and the royal abbey of Westminster. Now another thousand years on, with the turbulence and squalor of history transmuted into the more or less reverential awe and amazement at the Abbey's survival and at the extraordinary scenes it has staged, we are able to trace the roots of its confused magnificence back to the marshland of Bulinga Fen and the Roman need to cross it.

Over that first thousand years the anonymity which seems proper for wastelands is pushed back. The tributary is the Ey-Burn— the island stream—, or Teo-Burn—boundary stream—later the Tyburn, flowing from Mary le Bourne down to Marble Arch, the site of Tyburn, place of execution, then by what is now Brook Street, Conduit Street, the dip in Piccadilly, through Green Park, dividing at Bulinga Fen into one branch which finds the Thames at Vauxhall Bridge by way of Victoria and Tachbrook Street, another by St James's Park to Thorney Island. The way through the marsh is marked by lines of stakes leading to and from Tothill, a mound serving as a useful marker. Thorney names its own encircling water courses: Merseflete to the north, Mill Ditch to the south, and Long Ditch connecting them on the west. Downstream, at the narrows, London Bridge offers a dry though longer route across the river. Along the hard strand between here and Thorney a trading settlement of wharves—Lundenvic—lines the river. And Bramble Island, at least once the thorns are cleared, has potential. It is bounded by navigable streams. Building materials can easily be brought in. It has two springs on it, as well as the flow of the Ey-Burn to provide water and

Thorney Island, the site of Westminster Abbey, may have connected Roman Watling Street with Dover Street by means of a ford across the wide shallow River Thames.

The most complete of the Abbey's 11th-century domestic buildings, the Norman Undercroft beneath the monks' dormitory, is now used as the Abbey Museum.

Found near the Abbey in Great College Street in 1958 this 2nd-century Roman boy holding a ball was probably a funerary sculpture.

St Peter arrives at Thorney Island by boat to consecrate in his name the church supposedly built there early in the 7th century AD (from the 13th-century manuscript *La Estoire de Seint Aedward le Roi*).

flush the drains. 'The great fish-bearing Thames' abounds in salmon, and oysters from the estuary can be carried up by boat on the flood tide. And though there is not a great deal of suitable building land — by the time of Domesday Book there are still only 25 houses recorded—the place invites occupation.

The accounts of the origins of Westminster Abbey are imaginatively appealing but from a historian's perspective entirely fanciful. But their power as legends has ensured their persistence, and they are intrinsic to the story. In the 2nd century AD, runs one account, the Roman Temple of Apollo on Thorney Island was destroyed by an earthquake, and in its place a native king, whose Roman name was Lucius, built the first church. Abandoned and reduced to ruins, its rebuilding is narrated in the second foundation myth. Early in the 7th century, Sebert, son of Sledd, a Saxon king of Essex, was converted to Christianity by Mellitus, Bishop of London, a friend of St Augustine, and refounded the church on Thorney. The old tale of the dedication of this building has provided the Abbey over the centuries with a cherished image of its highly favoured nativity. As with wine, the telling of such tales improves with age. Here is Ælred's version of 1163:

'On the very night before the dedication, a traveller appeared to a certain fisherman on the further bank of the river Thames. He offered his fare, and asked for a passage across, which he was granted. Stepping out of the boat he entered the church, as the fisherman watched, — and, lo, suddenly a heavenly light shone, and all was illuminated with amazing splendour, turning night into day. A multitude of the heavenly host passed in and out, and a heavenly

anthem resounded from a choir in procession. All was full of light, all suffused with joy. Hearing was enhanced with the glad song of angels; scent sated with an ineffable fragrance; sight dazzled with the radiance of heaven. Earth and heaven seemed conjoined; the human linked to the divine, and angels were seen as on Jacob's ladder ascending and descending throughout the sacred ceremony. What then? When all the ceremonies fitting to dedicate a church had been carried out, the stranger returned to the fisherman. He found him terrified, dazzled by the divine light and all but senseless. With consoling words he brought the man to himself. They entered the skiff together, and the traveller asked "Have you anything to eat?" "I have caught nothing", the fisherman replied, "for I was overcome by the brilliance of the light, and was delayed waiting for you, but I was confident I would receive the fare you promised." "Now let down your nets for a catch," said the stranger. The fisherman did as he was instructed, and soon the net was full of a great quantity of fish. When they reached the shore, his passenger said: "Take this fish, which exceeds all others in size and worth, to Bishop Mellitus from me. The rest keep for yourself as the fare for my passage. I who speak to you am Peter, who with my fellow citizens have dedicated this church built in my honour, and by the authority of my holiness have forestalled the bishop's blessing. Tell Mellitus therefore what you have seen and heard, and the marks of dedication made on the walls will be evidence for your story." Next day, when Mellitus and Sebert arrived for the consecration, they found the fragrance of heavenly incense and the wax of heavenly candles. Accepting such holy signs, they held a thanksgiving service before dining on the fisherman's salmon.'

Both accounts appear to be popular mythologisations of the conversion to Christianity of pagan rulers. It is impossible to say when they were shaped, but from the late 11th century, when the monk Sulcard wrote them down, they were repeated and embellished by historians and chroniclers for 500 years in an extended game of

Edric the Fisherman, who rowed St Peter to Thorney Island, was rewarded with a huge catch of salmon. Here he presents the largest to Mellitus, Bishop of London. The episode is re-enacted each year at the Abbey's St Peter's Day feast (*La Estoire de Seint Aedward le Roi*).

The consecration of a church: an illumination in the Litlyngton Missal, commissioned by Abbot Nicholas Litlyngton in 1383–4.

The supposed tomb of King Sebert, a 7th-century king of Essex, claimed by later chroniclers to be the founder of the Abbey. In the 14th century the monks conveniently 'discovered' his tomb in the Cloisters, and translated the body to a new tomb beneath the Sedilia, in the South Ambulatory.

Chinese whispers until the legends set hard. The foundation myths of religious houses owed more to ecclesiastical politics than to historical truth, and forgers of documents in the 11th and 12th centuries, especially skilled at Westminster, unwittingly laid booby-traps for future historians. For example, the protracted rivalry for precedence between Westminster and Glastonbury Abbeys led to a series of claims leap-frogging back into history until Glastonbury flourished the trump card of Joseph of Arimathaea and the Holy Grail to snatch a bold but improbable foundation date in the 1st century AD.

Sulcard's story of the 11th century connects the foundation with Ethelbert, King of Kent, and mentions only an anonymous 'wealthy citizen' as the founder. Goscelin's Life of St Mellitus repeats Sulcard's version, which is then passed to William of Malmesbury about 1120. But in Osbert de Clare's Life of St Edward, written about 1140, Sebert, a quite new name, is substituted for the unknown citizen, and the tithe of salmon arrives in the story, together with the idea that the motive for the premature consecration by St Peter was the exclusion of the Bishop of London from jurisdiction over the Abbey. The consequences of this clerical rivalry linger to this day, when the Bishop of London is required to seek the formal permission of the Dean and Chapter of Westminster to enter the Abbey precinct. Osbert, whom we shall encounter again in the murky process of securing the canonisation of Edward the Confessor, succeeded in foisting his version of the foundation upon subsequent chroniclers. Accretions continued at least until 1440 when, in the *Liber Regius*, the fisherman is christened Edric, and as late as Stow's *Chronicles* [1580], the overthrowing of the Temple of Apollo in AD 153 is solemnly juxtaposed with the entry 'wolves destroyed'. The 14th-century discovery of the alleged grave of King Sebert in the cloisters by the monks and his translation to a place of honour on the south side of the sacrarium within the Abbey was a notable attempt to consolidate the myth.

The search for a firm footing in history is unrewarded until the middle of the 10th century. The Venerable Bede had mentioned the foundation of St Paul's, but not St Peter's. A charter dated AD 785 had confirmed the grant of land at Aldenham to the monastery of St Peter by Offa, King of Mercia, but is thought to be a very early forgery. Its description of Thorney as 'locus terribilis' may refer to its sacredness rather than its savagery. There may have been a small minster church by the end of the 8th century, served by canons, then members of a religious community with pastoral responsibilities, for how else would Westminster have been so named, but if so, then successive Danish raids between 835 and 872, when they stayed, would probably have laid it waste. Though Alfred the Great recaptured London in 886, spasmodic warfare continued until the establishment of Canute's Danish dynasty in 1016.

King Edgar's Charter: 'First up from Thames', draws the boundaries of Westminster.

†Anno abincarnaaone ðñi bionir numir quandam parta

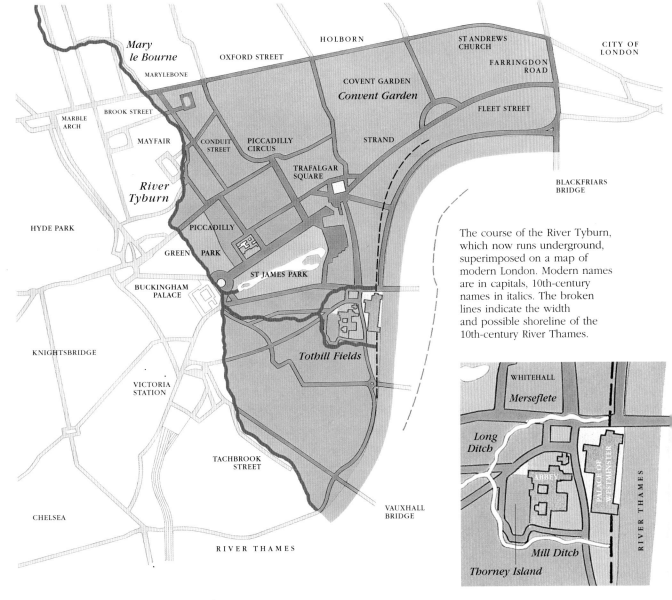

The course of the River Tyburn, which now runs underground, superimposed on a map of modern London. Modern names are in capitals, 10th-century names in italics. The broken lines indicate the width and possible shoreline of the 10th-century River Thames.

Thorney Island's encircling water courses: Merseflete to the north, Mill Ditch to the south, and Long Ditch in the west.

But, in the reign of King Edgar, from 957 to 975, a movement of religious renewal, embodied in the *Regularis Concordia*, emerges from the Danish turbulence. The kingdom of England is established, and monastic life at Westminster undoubtedly begins. Dunstan had founded a Benedictine community at Glastonbury around 940. Under Edgar, he was concurrently Bishop of Worcester and London, and then Archbishop of Canterbury, and either while Bishop of London (959–60) or as Archbishop in the early 970s, he founded Westminster with monks transferred from Glastonbury. Thorneia was bought from the King, for 'restoration of ruined chapels and setting up the institutions of the monastery'.

A Charter of King Edgar, wrongly dated 951, draws the boundaries of Westminster, rescuing it from the viscosity of swamp, tidal creek and mud, as if creating a theatre which it challenges the future to fill. 'First up from Thames, along Merfleet to Pollen-stock, so to Bulinga Fen; afterwards from the fen along the old ditch to Cowford. From Cowford up, along Tyburne to the broad military road: following the military road to the old stock of St Andrew's Church: then within London Fen, proceeding south on Thames to midstream; and along the stream, by land and strand, to Merfleet.' There is an echo here of Adam naming creatures in Eden; this is where things begin.

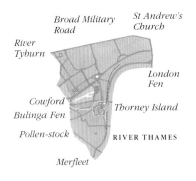

Pink marks the extent of Edgar's gift of land to Westminster

l又qui mutauit. y
tali sct Edmundi

nitate gaudent angeli.
filium di . P. Domi
Eusquih
transieum

The Rule of St Benedict, Abbot of Monte Cassino, drawn up in the 6th century, envisaged an enclosed community dependent for subsistence on income derived from land and alms. Westminster matches the pattern of earlier English Benedictine houses with their preference for fenland — Glastonbury, Peterborough, Ely — yet differed from them in a way that was to determine the ebb and flow of its destiny and see it transcend all other monastic houses in function and importance. From its earliest days it attracted royal patronage. The idea of a private abbey for royal use had precedents in Byzantine, Carolingian and Frankish lands: Ravenna, Aachen, St Denis. Now at Westminster Saxon and Danish kings were to emulate them. Edgar, Ethelred and Canute gave relics to St Dunstan's foundation. Athelstan gave part of the True Cross and Sepulchre, and portions of Mount Sinai and the Mount of Olives, though presumably not inconveniently large for the 'monasteriolum' (little monastery] recorded in 1050.

The royal bond was consolidated by Canute, the first king to establish on Thorney a residence that was soon to become the Palace of Westminster. Here he is said to have rebuked the tide of the wide and shifting Thames. (It is an irrelevant but pleasing reflection that in Canute's time a tidal creek reached—and halted at—the site of what is now Buckingham Palace.)

The names of the Saxon abbots give us our first sense of continuous life at Westminster: Wulfsige, Aelfwig, Wulfnoth, whose death is recorded in 1049 by the Anglo-Saxon Chronicle. Harold Harefoot, who succeeded Canute as Regent, then King, was the first royal burial in the Abbey in 1040, but his corpse enjoyed its preeminence only briefly before being thrown out, probably into the river, by Hartha canut, his successor. On Easter Day 1043 Edward the Confessor was crowned at Winchester. He appointed as Abbot of Westminster Eadwine, a personal friend whose rule was to span the building of the first great abbey church and the change of dynasty from Saxon to Norman in 1066. The scene is set for greatness.

Facing page:

An illuminated initial from the Litlyngton Missal (1383–4) illustrates Edward the Confessor enthroned, holding the ring from the pilgrim story (p.22).

A 20th-century window by Sir Ninian Comper in the North Nave Aisle depicts Eadwine, Abbot of Westminster under both Edward the Confessor and William the Conqueror.

The coronation of Edward the Confessor at Winchester Cathedral, 1043, illustrated in *Flores Historiarum*, a celebrated chronicle written by a monk chronicler, Matthew Paris, in the first half of the 13th century.

2.

Confessor and Conqueror

1045–1200

Ethelred, Edward's father, 'unready' (rash or impulsive) at the time of the incursions of barbarian Danes led by Sweyn and Canute, was exiled from his kingdom. So he caused his son to suffer for his faith (hence 'Confessor') by being deprived at an early age of his patrimony. Edward was brought up in Normandy and, though he was a Saxon king, the chief influences on him were Norman. 1066 was not the great divide beloved of those who prefer their history simple.

Alfred
(871–99)

Edward the Elder
(899–925)

Athelstan (925–39)   Edmund (939–46)   Eadred (946–55)

Eadwig (955–59)   Edgar (957–75)

Edward the Martyr (975–8)

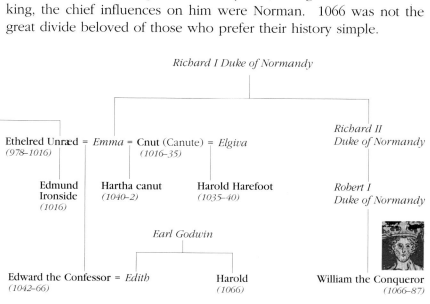

Richard I Duke of Normandy

Ethelred Unræd = *Emma* = Cnut (Canute) = *Elgiva*
(978–1016)   (1016–35)

Richard II Duke of Normandy

Edmund Ironside (1016)   Hartha canut (1040–2)   Harold Harefoot (1035–40)

Robert I Duke of Normandy

Earl Godwin

Edward the Confessor = *Edith* (1042–66)   Harold (1066)

William the Conqueror (1066–87)

The ruins of Romanesque Jumièges, near Rouen, a likely French prototype for Edward's Westminster Abbey.

In 1044, the year after his coronation, Edward summoned Robert, Abbot of Jumièges, the abbey on the Seine west of Rouen, to be Bishop of London and subsequently Archbishop of Canterbury. In the same year he must have taken a decision which ensured that London would become England's capital. This was to raise Westminster in magnificence for perpetuity by rebuilding it on a grand scale and by associating himself with it and establishing an adjacent palace and court. And as he turned to a Norman churchman for his bishop, he turned also to Norman architecture for his church. Jumièges was about to undergo a Romanesque reconstruction in dazzling white stone (1052–66); Westminster could and would better it.

There are four chief sources of information about Edward's life, two from the 11th century — the anonymous *Vita Ædwardi* completed within two years of his death, and Sulcard's History of Westminster, written a decade later — and two from the 12th century — by Osbert de Clare (1138) and Ælred of Rievaulx (1163). They are progressively more untrustworthy. Osbert's and Ælred's accounts are shaped by the context of the Confessor's canonisation, the first propagandist and the second celebratory. They belong to hagiography rather than history. And even with the earlier narratives, we must remember that medieval historians of the great and not so good would expect to write what was appropriate rather than what was strictly true. But true or not, they are part of the story, and in the absence of other sources, to them we must sceptically turn.

The *Vita Ædwardi* lists Edward's motives for founding a great Abbey church at Westminster: his piety and devotion to St Peter, the favourable situation of the place, on the river and close to London, but principally 'because he chose to have for himself a place of burial there'. It was to be financed by a tithe on the king's own possessions. Sulcard adds a further reason: Edward had vowed to make a pilgrimage to St Peter's tomb in Rome if he regained his kingdom, but his wish was opposed by his advisers who feared disorder in his absence. So a deputation was sent in his place, and he was released from his vow on condition that he founded or restored a monastery dedicated to St Peter.

There is a record of a gift of land from Ulf, the port-sheriff, and his wife in 1043 or 1044, and then the great work began in 1045. The *Vita Ædwardi* states that the new church was built far enough to the east of the existing one to enable services to continue in it; Sulcard that the older church was destroyed to make way for the new. By

Harold marched south from victory over the Norwegians at Stamford Bridge to be defeated at Hastings on October 14th 1066. This battle marked the Norman conquest of Saxon England.

1042 Edward the Confessor, King of England

1045 Building of the first Abbey begins.

December 28th 1065 Consecration of the Abbey

January 1066 Death and burial of Edward Harold crowned at Westminster

October 14th 1066 Battle of Hastings.

December 25th 1066 Coronation of William I

September 26th 1087 Coronation of William II

August 5th 1100 Coronation of Henry I

December 26th 1135 Coronation of Stephen

December 19th 1154 Coronation of Henry II

1161 Canonisation of the Confessor

1163 Translation of the saint's body to the first shrine

September 3rd 1189 Coronation of Richard I

May 27th 1199 Coronation of John

How Thorney Island may have looked at the close of the 11th century. Beyond the Abbey buildings are the Royal Palace and the eastern branch of the stream marking the boundary of the island. It enters the Thames where Westminster Bridge now spans the river.

The Confessor in life and death. On the right his body is carried to the newly consecrated Abbey for burial in January 1066. The Bayeux Tapestry, embroidered c. 1067–70 to chronicle the deeds of William the Conqueror, shows Edward's incomplete Romanesque church.

royal writ Teinfrith was named as the king's churchwright, and Godwin Greatsyd ('fat purse') as both mason and benefactor. The scale of the building, in Reigate stone, eclipsed anything built in England before. Excavation at intervals in the last 150 years, in the apse and nave, exposed pier plinths for ten bays, located a few feet within the piers of the later church, and closely resembling those at Jumièges. Its length, at 98.2 metres, made it bigger than all the major churches in Normandy. It was the first cruciform church in England, and its lantern tower and turrets must have amazed all who saw them. In the celebrated impression of Westminster on the Bayeux Tapestry, a comet is poised above the Abbey, holding the gaze of every bystander. But in 11th-century London, the Abbey was a comet in its own right:

'The sanctuary of the high altar rises up with very high vaults; it is made with square stones and even jointing, and is brought round in a curve. Then the crossing, which is to contain in the middle the choir of those who sing God's praises, and with its twofold abutment on either side to steady the lofty summit of the tower in the middle, rises simply at first with a low and sturdy vault, swells with many a spiral winding stair of elaborate article, but then with a plain wall reaches the wooden roof which is carefully covered with lead.' The author of the *Vita Ædwardi* is describing a wonder of the world.

In 1065 Edward kept Christmas at Westminster. His church was far enough advanced for its consecration. The Bayeux Tapestry depicts only five bays west of the crossing, and the completion may have taken until about 1080. But on Christmas Eve Edward was afflicted with a fever, the first in a chain of dramatic events leading, in a year and a day, to the coronation of William of Normandy in the Abbey on Christmas Day 1066. Edward, we are told, manfully concealed his sickness for three days so as not to sully the festivities, but on December 27th withdrew to his deathbed, giving orders that his church was to be dedicated on Holy Innocents' Day, December 28th. 'At Midwinter King Edward came to Westminster, and had the minster there consecrated,' baldly states the Saxon Chronicle. But the hallowing was no mean affair, attended by two archbishops, eight bishops and eight abbots. The list of relics possessed at the dedication is striking. It includes, given by the Confessor himself, the Virgin Mary's milk, hair, shoes and bed; hairs of St Peter''s beard; a great part of the body of

HERE THEY HAVE GIVEN THE
KING'S CROWN TO HAROLD

HERE SITS HAROLD THE
KING OF THE ENGLISH

THESE MEN MARVEL AT THE STAR (Halley's comet)

STIGAND ARCHBISHOP

HAROLD

St Buttulph the Abbot, and half a jaw with three teeth of St Anastasia. Such treasures were of no avail to Edward, who sank towards death. The *Vita Ædwardi* constructs a noble deathbed scene, in which he beseeches those sorrowing around him 'Do not weep, but intercede with God for my soul, and give me leave to go to Him.' He takes farewell of Edith, his wife, and Harold, her brother, and commands 'Let the grave for my burial be prepared in the minster in the place which shall be shown to you. Fear not, I shall not die now, but by God's mercy regain my strength.' And King Edward died on the eve of Twelfth Mass (January 5th) and was buried on the Twelfth Mass Day within the newly hallowed church, in a stone sarcophagus below the pavement in front of the high altar. 'Hic portatur corpus Eadwardi regis at ecclesiam Petri:' in the Bayeux Tapestry the coffin is borne by elongated figures towards the west end of the Abbey, while the hand of God points from the skies to the chosen burial place. On the day of Edward's burial, Harold was crowned.

Emphasis is placed on the comet as a sign of ill-omen even as Harold is acclaimed king in Westminster Abbey.

Five completed bays, elaborate Lantern tower, the placing of the weather vane and the hand of God set the seal on Edward's new Abbey, consecrated in December 1065, and depicted here in the Bayeux Tapestry.

Coronation of William I
in Westminster Abbey from
the *Chronica Majora* of
Matthew Paris.

The fading figure of Gilbert
Crispin, Abbot 1085–1117, moved
under a stone bench in the South
Cloister to save it from further
wear and tear.

Ten months later William of Normandy, claiming that Edward
had named him as his heir, landed at Pevensey, and, in battle at
Hastings, Harold was slain. William, now Conqueror reached London
in December, and for reasons that blend the personal with the politic,
visited the Abbey, where he offered 50 marks of silver and rich palls
for the altar and Edward's tomb. On Christmas Day 1066, in emulation of Charlemagne, he was crowned at Westminster, the first in a line
of thirty-nine succeeding kings and queens. In a piece of symbol-
ism both deferential and triumphant he was crowned at the crossing
beneath the central tower on a spot directly above the buried Edward.
The Bishop of Coutances presented William to the people, and called
on them in French, and Aldred, Archbishop of York in English, to
acclaim him king. The acclamation, a French ritual, became integrated
into the English Coronation service down to the present day. Aldred,
a good and eloquent man, addressed the English with well-chosen
words; he asked whether it was their wish that William should be
crowned as their king. Without the slightest hesitation they all proclaimed their joyful assent, with one mind and one voice, as though
inspired by heaven. But the armed and mounted guards who had
been posted outside the Abbey, mistakenly thought that the roar of
acceptance was a sign of treachery, and recklessly began to set fire to
the city. William is said to have sat trembling while the ritual was suspended, but if so it is a surprising facet of his character. Holinshed's
version of events 500 years later reveals delightfully how the whispers
of medieval history culminate in a gossip column. William was
crowned 'by Aldred Archbishop of Yorke. For he would not receive
the crowne at the hands of Stigand archbishop of Canterbury because
he was hated, and furthermore judged to be a very lewd person and
a naughtie liver.' Disorder inside the Abbey or beyond was a common
feature of rough and ready early coronations. On the day of Richard
I's coronation in 1189, 'a sacrifice of the Jews to their father, the Devil,
was commenced in the city of London, and so long was the duration
of this famous mystery, that the holocaust could scarcely be accom-
plished the ensuing day.' Ten years later, so the chronicler Roger of
Wendover wanted posterity to believe, King John convulsed with
laughter at the lawless conduct of his associates, dropped a spear and
rushed away without receiving the sacrament.

After the Conquest, the pre-eminence of Norman churchmen
at Westminster was naturally unquestioned. Geoffrey, Abbot of
Jumièges, was appointed Abbot of Westminster in 1071 or 1072, after
the death of the Saxon Eadwine, and in about 1085 Gilbert Crispin was
chosen: he was from Bec, where Lanfranc had been Abbot until 1063,
and where he and Anselm, both to become Archbishops of
Canterbury, formed a lasting friendship. But it was the last Saxon
bishop, Wulfstan of Worcester, threatened with dismissal because of
his native tongue, who was at the centre of a supposed miracle in the
Abbey which accelerated a movement that brought the buried
Edward back to haunt his Norman successors for a century. The story
goes that Wulfstan, seeking justice from his former lord, the
Confessor, declared that he would surrender his pastoral staff to none

HARO L D·REX·INTERFEC
TVS·EST

but him. He laid the staff upon the stone marking Edward's tomb; here it took root and proved immovable, until the royal command assured Wulfstan of his bishopric, and he was then able to take back his crozier.

The omens for the Confessor's sanctity had been encouraging even at the deathbed, where was seen in his dead body 'the glory of a soul departing to God. For the flesh of his face blushed like a rose. The adjacent beard gleamed like a lily, his hands, laid out straight, whitened.' Such episodes as Edward's deathbed transfiguration and Wulfstan's crozier, compounded by rumours of miracles at the tomb — cures of a blind bell-ringer and a hunchback — were made the pretext for the opening of the tomb in 1102, thirty-seven years after Edward's burial, in the presence of Henry I. When the top slab was removed, a sweet fragrance filled the church, and the body was found whole and in no way decomposed. Gundulf, Bishop of Rochester, released the head and beard from the pall, and tried to pull out a hair from the beard, but refrained when rebuked

'HAROLD REX INTERFECTUS EST': King Harold is Killed.

King Harold's death and defeat on October 14th 1066 at the battle of Hastings, as depicted in the Bayeux Tapestry. William of Normandy, the Conqueror, rode on to London, where he was crowned on Christmas Day 1066. Since then England has never been successfully invaded.

One of the few surviving sculptures from Edward the Confessor's Abbey. This carved capital, from the 11th or early 12th century, illustrates the Judgement of Solomon, in which he adjudicates between two women both claiming to be the mother of the same baby.

13th-century tile in the Chapter House: Edward the Confessor giving his ring to John the Evangelist disguised as a beggar.

by Abbot Crispin. Then they shut up in the sepulchre the holy body that they had found completely intact, and replaced 'Wulfstan's slab'.

Now our only authority for the details of this remarkable sign of Edward's sanctity is Osbert de Clare, writing in 1138. He is extremely unlikely to have been present in 1102. Osbert is clearly one of those indispensably energetic but spiky people with or without whom any society finds it hard to get along. As Prior of Westminster in the early 1120s, he was indignant both at the decay of the monastic community, and at the royal court, which he stigmatised as 'the Babylonish Furnace'. Predictably, he was suspended and banished ('sent to Ely') for ten years. On his return in 1134 he seems to have undertaken single-handedly, with prodigious energy, the aim of securing Edward's canonisation. The supposed miracles increased in frequency after his return from Ely, and his Life of Edward (1138), rhetorically elevates and embellishes every scrap of evidence. Deeply devoted to Westminster, and also smarting from a sense of personal wrong, he was determined that the Abbey, both as a royal shrine and as St Peter's chosen home, must enjoy exemption from episcopal interference. The best guarantee of such independence was the possession of a royal saint. So he set about rewriting the Abbey's early history, making himself the centre of the production line for forged documents that Westminster became in his time. The charters of Dunstan and Edgar, the diplomas of the Conqueror and Henry I all contain Osbert's favourite phrases; he invents Sebert's royal connection with the Abbey's foundation. (In general, the purpose of such forgery, widespread in monasteries, was to enhance status rather than make false claims.) At no point was there any evidence that the cause of canonisation was fuelled by a strong popular cult; fifteen years after Edward's death, according to Sulcard, the monks were not sure where his tomb was. But Osbert's snowball rolled on, picking up ever-new stories. One of these, to become a dominant subject of the decoration of Henry III's building, was the fairy tale story of the King and the beggar.

Edward, on his way to the dedication of the Chapel of St John the Evangelist at Clavering, was greeted by a beggar imploring alms. There being no gold or silver in his chest, the King took from his own hand his ring, which he gave to the beggar, who vanished. Soon afterwards two English pilgrims from Ludlow, stranded by night in Syria, were met by an old man with lighted tapers. They told him of their king and country, at which the old man guided them to shelter, introduced himself as the Evangelist, and gave them the royal ring to carry back to Edward, with the message that within six months he would meet St John in Paradise.

Miracles there may have been, but in the end it was *realpolitik* that persuaded Pope Alexander III to act. In 1160 Henry II backed him to resolve the Papal schism, and the Bull of Canonisation was promptly issued on February 7th 1161. For two further years Henry was abroad, but in 1163 the translation of St Edward took place on October 13th, in the presence of Archbishop Thomas Becket, who claimed Wulfstan's slab from the superseded tomb as his bounty. In a ceremony glorifying Christian kingship, the king and his chief nobles carried the feretory—a chest with openings for seeing and touching the lead coffin within—in procession through the cloisters to the new shrine, in the same position as the former tomb, but above the ground. A private royal cult now ensured the Abbey's unique status.

Thomas Becket was not the only turbulent priest to trouble Henry II. At a time bristling with ecclesiastical jealousies and rivalries, the king often found himself the unwilling focus for the squabbles of his volatile prelates. In 1154 the Abbot of the appropriately named Abbey of Battle, suspecting that the Bishop of Chichester had secured the king's agreement not to validate a (forged) charter granting the abbey exemption from episcopal authority, decided to confront Henry when he went to hear mass at Westminster. He waited near the altar, and after the introit challenged the king to reverse his decision. Henry called over his chancellor and told him to fix the royal seal to the abbot's charter. But suddenly up came the Bishop 'at a near run' to put his case: negotiations lasted until the 'Pax Domini', the priest's greeting before communion. This involved no longer a kiss, as in the early church, but the passing round of a cross or 'pax-board'. The bishop received the pax from the priest, next offered it to the king, and then 'to the amazement of many', to the Abbot of Battle. It was a brief peace; the dispute continued.

There was a less happy outcome to the battle of the primates, which took place in St Catherine's Chapel, in the Infirmary, in 1176, when the Council of Westminster gathered around Cardinal Hugo Pierleone, the Papal Legate. Richard, Archbishop of Canterbury, sat at the cardinal's right hand, 'as in his proper place. In springs Roger Archbishop of York, and finding Canterbury so seated, fairly sits him down on Canterbury's lap—a baby too big to be danced thereon; yea, Canterbury's servants dandled this large child, plucked him from thence and buffeted him to purpose', breaking his mitre and tearing his cope. 'The cardinal fled, and hid himself from their sight, and matters were so impeded that no council was held. Each of them complained to the Lord king about the injuries done to him.'

'The two only inconveniences of London', writes Roger Fitzstephen in his contemporary description of the city, 'are the excessive drinking of some foolish people, and the frequent fires.' He had obviously missed the Council of Westminster.

William I, William II, Henry I and Stephen, each claiming kinship with the Abbey, from the *Chronica Majora* of Matthew Paris.

The wax seal of St Peter's Westminster, of the early 13th century.

Henry and one of his masons

3.

Henry III and the Glory of Westminster

1200–1298

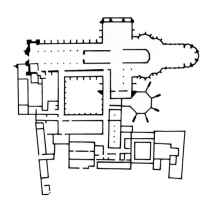

The section of the Abbey rebuilt in the 13th century by Henry III.

Head of a young prince: a painted wooden carving on the Sedilia, to the right of the High Altar.

Edward's canonisation had bestowed a patron saint on the royal line. It was indeed a gift from heaven, to be thus able to underpin with sanctity an elevated conception of kingship. In the 13th century Henry III, who came to the throne in 1216, at the age of 9, and occupied it for fifty-six years, was to become obsessed with the cult of the Confessor. His obsession was to initiate the most ambitious church building project medieval Europe had seen, and to transform the first great Romanesque church in England into the greatest French Gothic one. The Abbey we know today is essentially Henry III's achievement, though, because of the destructiveness of the religious and political revolutions of later centuries, a pale shadow of his creation.

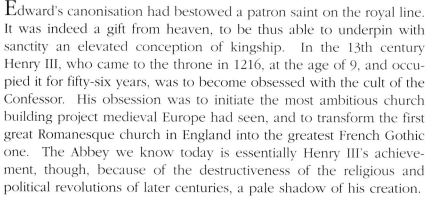

William the Conqueror
(1066–87)

William II
(1087–1100)

Adela = Stephen Count of Blois

Stephen
(1135–54)

Henry I = *Matilda*
(1100–35)

Geoffrey Plantagenet = **Mathilda**
Count of Anjou   *(declared Queen 1135)*

Henry II
(1154–89)

Richard I
(1189–99)

John
(1199–1216)

Henry III
(1216–72)

Sources for the events of this period are more dependable. Matthew Paris, an engaging chronicler based at St Albans, was often at Westminster and reported what he saw. Detailed accounts survive from the rebuilding of the Abbey: tradesmen's names and transactions flesh out the day-to-day labour of the vast slow enterprise. A narrator of the Abbey's history feels, for the first time, that he is standing on firm ground.

Three apostles: a detail from the 13th-century Retable.

1216
Coronation of Henry III at Gloucester

1220
Foundation of first Lady Chapel coronation of Henry III at Westminster

1245
Rebuilding of the Abbey begins

October 13th 1269
Consecration of the Abbey and translation of the Confessor to new shrine

August 19th 1274
Coronation of Edward I.

1296
Stone of Scone entrusted to the Abbey.

As with the Confessor's church, the origins of Henry's are to be found in France. A prodigious period of French Gothic architecture had begun in 1144 at St Denis, which was both a royal necropolis and the home of the French coronation regalia. Notre-Dame, Reims, Troyes, Auxerre and Amiens followed, between 1180 and 1241. A spirit of rivalry with these French consecrations was sharpened when the loss of Anjou to the French in 1204 deprived the English kings of their mausoleum at Fontevraud. Henry, although sometimes described as the first truly English king, looked to France with mixed feelings of kinship and emulation. He had no doubts about adopting the French style as his architectural model, but was intent on surpassing it too. Reims, the French coronation church, was dedicated in 1241; Henry was in France in 1242 and 1243; later he visited Sainte Chapelle, consecrated under Louis IX in 1248 as a reliquary church for which the French king had assumed responsibility after taking part in the procession there of the Crown of Thorns. Reliquary, regalia, coronation, mausoleum: why should these not be combined in England in one glorious building which was already the shrine of the royal saint?

Henry's reign had a precarious beginning. King John's death through a surfeit of new cider and peaches brought a 9-year-old to the throne. He is the only king to have been crowned twice: the first time at Gloucester in 1216, when London could not be safely gained and his nobles were eager to establish the legitimacy of the

Henry III holding the new Abbey, from the *Chronica Majora* of Matthew Paris

succession. On May 16th 1220 he observed the Vigil of Pentecost in the Abbey, and laid the foundation stone of Abbot Humez's Lady Chapel, built in response to the popular cult of the Virgin spreading rapidly across Europe under the influence of the earlier preaching of St Bernard of Clairvaux. The next day Henry, now 13, was crowned a second time by Stephen Langton, Archbishop of Canterbury. 'The archbishop demanded from king Henry the oath, namely that he would protect the church of God, guard the peace of both clergy and people, and uphold the good laws of the kingdom. And so when the oath had been sworn, the archbishop bestowed on the king, who had not yet completed his thirteenth year, the insignia of royalty and the crown of the most saintly king Edward. That coronation of the king was indeed conducted with such great order and splendour, that those among the older nobles of England asserted that they could not recall any of the king's predecessors ever being crowned with such a degree of concord and tranquillity.' (The Jews, however, were kept in the Tower of London as a precaution.) 'As a sign of rejoicing', records Matthew Paris, 'an edict went out that all except the clergy should wear garlands of flowers.' Henry's bond with Westminster was made.

In 1241 he gave the first of the orders leading to the re-creation of the building, 'a magnificent shrine to be made out of purest refined gold and precious stones, to be constructed in London by the most skilled goldsmiths, for the deposition of the relics of the blessed Edward'. Matthew Paris heard him solemnly declare that he had paid out more than one hundred thousand marks for the glorious king and blessed Confessor's entombment. The paradigms of the great French cathedrals, the primary influence on Henry's motivation, had been supplemented in the early years of his reign by two English precedents: the popularity of Thomas Becket's shrine at Canterbury, the dedication of which in 1224 the young king had witnessed, and the magnificence of the cathedral at Salisbury then under construction. So Henry was now ready to make the major commitment, both financial and spiritual, of his kingship. In December 1243, after Henry's return from France, Master Henry of Reynes received his gown of office as Master of the King's Masons.

The king 'caused the greater part of the Conventual Church of the Blessed Peter to be pulled down, beginning on the day week after the Feast of the Apostles Peter and Paul.' On July 6th 1245 began the extraordinary enterprise of demolishing a huge and solidly built structure less than 200 years old, which had just been enriched by a Lady Chapel to the east of the high altar. A project so daring and so unnecessary could have been driven only by an undeviating royal will: to Westminster were brought Kentish ragstone, Caen and Reigate freestone, clunch (chalk) for filling the vaults, marble from the quarries at

At his second coronation in 1220 the 13-year-old Henry was crowned by Stephen Langton, Archbishop of Canterbury. This marginal sketch is from Matthew Paris's *Chronica Majora*.

Facing page: The Chapel of St Edward the Confessor, his shrine in the centre, encircled by the tombs of Henry III, Edward I and Queen Eleanor of Castile, Edward III and Queen Philippa of Hainault, Richard II and Queen Anne of Bohemia.

The Confessor's new shrine. In this drawing by Matthew Paris Edward can be seen offering his ring to St John the Evangelist disguised as a beggar. Pilgrims kneel before the golden feretory housing the Saint's body.

The head of the gilt-bronze effigy of Henry III, creator of the 13th-century Abbey

Henry III supervises work in progress on St Albans Abbey: a vivid scene of church building drawn by Matthew Paris.

Purbeck, timber from Kent, Essex and Berkshire, lead from Derbyshire to Boston by land, Boston to Westminster by water; seven orders of craftsmen: stone-cutters and masons, carpenters, marblers, polishers, smiths, plumbers, glaziers; over 400 workmen in high summer, falling to around 100 in mid-winter; Roger of Reigate, James the joiner, Adam the timber merchant, Richard the lime-burner, Peter the painter; to John Stoil for two hundredweight of osiers for scaffolding: 12*s.* 6*d.*; to William the swineherd for carting 1058 cartloads of sand: 21*s.* 2*d.* Henry of Reynes, master mason, directed the works until 1253; John of Gloucester until 1260, and then Robert of Beverley did a heroic span of 24 years, by which time Henry was dead, and the first phase of building came to an exhausted and penniless halt.

The financial challenge was colossal. The King's Treasury provided 3,000 marks (now about £700,000) a year. Every available source of funds was unscrupulously diverted to the keepers of the works: writs of liberate, issues of the great seal, fines and debts, fees for the granting of royal charters. In 1250 relaxation of a year's penance was granted for all 'who lent a helping hand to the fabric of the church of wonderful beauty being built at Westminster'. Henry was indifferent to the grousing of the populace provoked by his establishing St Edward's Fair at Westminster, intended to swell revenues for a full fifteen days, with no other fairs to be kept at the same time. 'Not without great trouble and paines to the citizens, which had not roome there, but in booths and tents, to their great disquieting and disease, for want of necessarie provision, being turmoiled too pitifullie in mire and dirt, through occasion of raine that

fic collato. memoria donatiouf indelebi
liter perpetuetur. Et hoc tali largitate op
anuit condicoue. ut de regno Anglie nlls
publice penitenf pro execucoe fibi iunne

Willegodum. Q̃ interpretat̄ volenf bonū.
Yere em̄ vir bone fuit uoluntatif. et de
stirpe regñ omniū. regeq̃ offe g̃sangui
tate propinq̃. Qui eū iuenem̃ ad

fell in that unseasonable time of the year. Besides this, the king took victuals and wine, where any could be found, and paid nothing for it.' The 'vox pop' of ordinary English life sounds querulously down the centuries. In 1267 Henry was so short of cash that he had to pawn the jewels of the still unfinished shrine, valued at £2,555, but they were redeemed in time for the consecration two years later.

Henry was impatient. In 1247, when the new work was scarcely begun, he sought to outdo Louis IX's Crown of Thorns with a crystalline reliquary of Christ's blood, newly arrived from the Holy Land, and authenticated by testimonial letters from the Patriarch of Jerusalem, the masters of the Templars and Hospitallers, and the bishops and archbishops of the Holy Land. The king kept vigil on St Edward's Eve, and then next day took part in a procession of all the priests of London from St Paul's to St Peter's. 'He carried (the reliquary) above his head for all to see, going on foot, humbly clad in a modest cloak without a hood. He walked without stopping all the way to Westminster Abbey. [In fact he had intended to go barefoot but was afraid that he might stumble and fall while gazing at this awesome and venerable treasure as he bore it aloft.] It should also be mentioned that he carried the flask in both hands, and even when the way was rough or uneven, he always kept his eyes fixed either on heaven or on the reliquary itself. The canopy, however, was carried on four spears, and two assistants supported the arms of the king in case his strength should falter through such strenuous exertion.' At Westminster the Bishop of Norwich celebrated mass for an overflowing crowd, and observed in his sermon that this relic would be venerated more in England than in Syria, which was now almost abandoned and desolate, since faith and piety were universally known to flourish more in England than in any other part of the world.

Henry had wanted the Abbey to be ready for its consecration on St Edward's Day, October 13th 1255, just ten years after the inauguration of the work. But both the scale of the task and financial squeezes caused delay. The Chapter House, the detached belfry, and the re-roofing and raising of the walls of the recent Lady Chapel to fit in with the new building all diverted labour and money from the main structure. By 1259 the transepts, apse, crossing and Chapter House were complete, and work west of the crossing began with the demolition of the monks' choir. Here five bays were constructed, reaching a point one bay west of the present organ screen. In the choir aisles of these bays, a wall decoration of stone armorial

Henry III's French Gothic reconstruction ended one bay west of the present organ screen. Work on the rest of the Nave was not resumed until 1376, and not completed until 1517. Here the join of older and newer work is clearly visible.

A 13th-century 'boss' — the keystone of a vault — with its original colour, showing a contest between a man and a man-beast. This is one of three in the Muniment Room, in the South Transept.

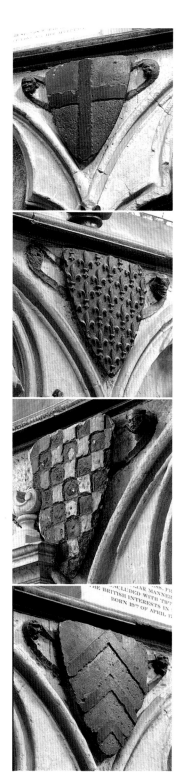

Heraldic stone shields hanging from grotesque heads line the North and South Quire Aisles of Henry III's 13th-century Abbey.

Facing page: The Queen and the Duke of Edinburgh walk through the Quire at their Golden Wedding service, on November 20th 1997.

shields, hanging by stone straps from grotesque heads, imitated a decorative detail in the hall where Henry had dined with Louis IX in Paris in 1254.

At last in 1269 the new quire was finished, and the long-delayed consecration could be celebrated. Looking now at his creation, Henry could identify all its French features: the rose windows and flying buttresses; the ambulatory around the apse with radiating side chapels, as at Reims; the north portal (at Westminster the state entrance because of its spatial relationship to the palace) copied from Amiens; the Chapter House echoing those at both Amiens and the Sainte Chapelle. Yet nowhere in France were so many wonders in combination. And nowhere in France was there to be found the rare quality of Italian craftsmanship applied to the finer decorative details of the interior. One hundred and fifty years earlier, Abbot Gilbert Crispin had secured a papal bull exempting the monastery from all episcopal rule and authority except that of Rome. The tireless worrying — and forging — of Osbert de Clare had strengthened the Abbey's claim to independence. A considerable, and costly disadvantage of this privilege was the need for each newly elected abbot to travel to Rome for confirmation. Abbot Richard of Ware was elected in 1258; at his leisure he journeyed twice to Rome, and at his leisure returned in 1268, with materials for the great pavement before the high altar, and a craftsman in inlaid marble ('cosmati' work), Petrus Odericus or Odensius, to set the polished stone and glass into a base of Purbeck marble in grave unearthly patterns of circles, hexagons and spirals, echoing but far surpassing the 'labyrinths' on the floors of French cathedrals. Cosmati decoration was applied also to the new shrine in its own chapel east of the high altar, and subsequently to the pavement of that chapel and to the tomb of Henry himself on the north side of it. Inlaid too were the spiralling marble pillars flanking the shrine — another decorative detail from Rome — supporting golden statues of the Confessor and St John as pilgrim.

The king had waited twenty-five years for this day, and had spent £41,248 (now £14.5m.) on the building, and over £5,000 (£1.8m.) more on the shrine. So, on 'the xiii daye of October, the kynge lette translate with great solempnytie the holy body of seynt Edwarde kynge and confessour, that before laye in the side of the quere, into the chapell at the back of the hygh aulter of Westmester abbey, and there layde it in a ryche shryne. For the kynge grievid that the relics of saint Edward were poorly enshrined and lowly, resolved that so great a luminary should not be buried, but be placed high as on a candlestick to enlighten the church.'

Also high on view for the consecration was the Retable, the ornate and exquisitely painted altarpiece depicting Christ in Majesty, St Peter, scenes of miracles and perhaps in a panel defaced in 1778, Edward the Confessor. It was rediscovered in a decaying state in 1725 doing lowly duty as the top of a cupboard housing wax effigies. Now on view in the South Ambulatory, it is the Abbey's greatest single treasure. It continues to proclaim the glory both of Henry III's creation and

Above: Christ in Majesty, from the central panel of the Retable.

Above right: Detail of Christ holding the World in His palm.

This and facing page: Details from the surviving left-hand section of the Retable, the 13th century altarpiece rediscovered in 1725 patching a cupboard housing effigies. It is now in the South Ambulatory.

Facing page: St Peter from the Retable.

Below: The healing Christ, part of The Raising of Jairus' Daughter.

the magnificence of a native artistic tradition of which it is the sole survivor, radiant in its ruins. Its miraculous impaired endurance distils the entire history of Westminster Abbey.

Work continued up to Henry's death in 1272, and beyond, and was described as 'fully finished' to the end of the quire in 1285. His intention had been to alter the western part of the building in keeping with the new work. In his will of 1253 he had included an injunction to his son Edward to complete the church of the Blessed Edward after whom he was named. But Edward I, who had seen Westminster Abbey suck his father's treasury dry, was doubtless relieved to let the burden drop. The accidents of history were to delay the complete fulfilment of Henry's vision for over two hundred years.

Another irksome and persistent disadvantage of being a royal church hard by the palace was that politics were continually leaning

The Cosmati work pavement in the Sacrarium, before the High Altar. It was created for the Abbey's consecration in 1269, and may have been a gift from the Pope to Abbot Ware. Its mysterious patterning includes a symbolic expression of the age of the world.

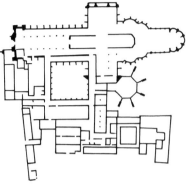

Abbey plan marking the position of the Cosmati Pavement.

The Cosmati Pavement covers much of the Sacrarium floor. Hidden under carpet for many years, it has now been uncovered and a programme of careful cleaning and conservation is under way.

upon the monastic community. In 1246 Richard of Croxley, Archdeacon of Westminster and a great friend of the king, was unanimously elected abbot, for the monks were afraid that if they acted otherwise, the king, who was their special patron, might leave unfinished their already half-demolished church. The refectory was used for the Council of State in 1244, and the fine new Chapter House became the regular meeting place of the House of Commons soon after its completion. Strife at the heart of the kingdom beset Westminster on St Edward's Day 1262 when Simon de Montfort, brother-in-law to the king, read to the Commons a document he had secured from Pope Urban IV asserting that the financial Provisions of Oxford were still binding on Henry, despite an earlier exemption. Shortly afterwards Henry was humiliatingly captured by de Montfort at Lewes, and compelled to make terms with him, before a reversal of fortunes saw Simon killed at Evesham in 1265. The rampant lion of Simon de Montfort's stone shield on the wall of the North Quire aisle, suspended from disembodied heads, is a *memento mori* to political fortune and human ambition.

It is as if the energies which had focused on the Abbey and driven up its lofty vaulting had spent themselves. The change of king was herald to a new order. Though Edward I and Eleanor of Castile were the first king and queen to be jointly crowned, in 1274, Edward's interest shifted to St Stephen's Chapel, in the Palace of Westminster, which he rebuilt and endowed from 1292 as if in rivalry. He made an unpropitious appearance at Convocation in the Refectory in 1294, demanding of the religious houses a subsidy of one-half of their possessions, at which, according to Matthew of Westminster, the Dean of St Paul's dropped dead at the king's feet. After his triumph over the Scots at the Battle of Dunbar in 1296, he seized the regalia and Stone of Scone, the coronation seat of the Kings of Scotland from Scone Palace, and entrusted them to Westminster. But this brief favour was soon squandered. Two disasters within five years were to destroy much of the monastery and alienate the king.

Abbot's head from the Sedilia

Facing page: The Sedilia, on the south side of the Sacrarium before the High Altar, where monks serving at Mass would sit during the service. It was completed in the early 14th century, and includes two surviving painted figures of kings on the panels, and the carved wooden heads of an abbot and two princes.

Far left: Simon de Montfort's shield in the North Quire Aisle. Henry III and the nobleman were at strife after 1262 and de Montfort was killed in battle before the Abbey was consecrated. But his shield remained in place.

Left: Reversed shield indicating the death of de Montfort from Matthew Paris's *Chronica Majora*.

The Three Kings and the Christ child from the Litlyngton Missal.

Courts and Kings

1298-1485

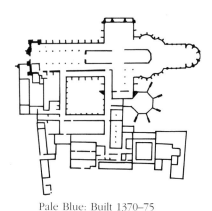

Pale Blue: Built 1370–75
Dark Blue: Building started 1376

The century of the Abbey's glory ended with ruins. The heat of a royal neighbour was inconveniently turned on the monastery in 1298 when, on March 29th, a day when Edward I arrived at the Palace of Westminster, a fire lit to greet him got out of control, burnt the smaller hall and surrounding rooms and, fanned by an east wind, spread to the Abbey. 'Divine grace' saved the church and Chapter House, but was insufficient to protect all the domestic buildings 'which were reduced to charcoal and ashes', record the Monastic Annals (though it was probably in the Abbey's interest for the damage to be exaggerated). In any event, the slow task of reconstruction of the ancillary buildings was to delay once again the rebuilding of the Romanesque Nave. And medieval delays tended to be measured in decades or even centuries.

So to sink into royal displeasure could not have happened at a less fortunate time. But the most notorious of all medieval burglaries, on April 24th 1303, was to cast a damning light upon the monks' conduct. From 1298 to 1303, Edward I's household was based in York. In the king's absence, slackness sidled in at Westminster. John Skenche and William of the Palace, 'heritary keeper' and his assistant, were given to revelry, in which some of the monks habitually joined. Richard of Pudlicott, merchant, arrested in Flanders as a surety for Edward I's debts there, escaped from prison and returned with a grudge. He joined the Palace merrymakers, on the pretext of seeking legal redress for his property forfeit in Flanders. He first helped himself to monastic silver from the refectory and then, having got away with that appropriation, turned his attention to the royal treasury, a branch of which had been billeted on the monastery in the belief that it was secure. Edward had obtained the crypt beneath the Chapter House as a store for the Royal Wardrobe, consisting primarily of jewels and plate. It was near the Abbey sacristy (now St Faith's Chapel) and may have been intended as a strongroom linked with it. But the Sacrist, Adam of Warfield, was a festive companion of Pudlicott.

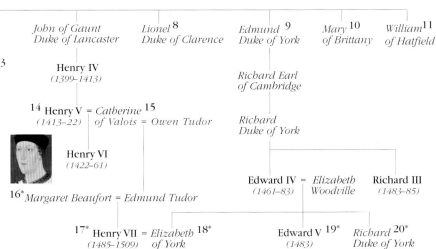

St Edward's Chapel contains the Shrine of Edward the Confessor, and the tombs of six kings and four queens.

ST EDWARD (THE CONFESSOR'S) CHAPEL

Edward the Confessor's Shrine

2a

14a

14

15 above

6, 7, 8, 9, 10, 11

2a Edward I's Coronation Chair

6, 7, 8, 9, 10, 11 Six of Edward III's fourteen children appear as weepers (mourners) on the south side of his tomb.

14a Henry V's Chantry Chapel

*16, 17, 18, 19, 20 Buried in Henry VII's Chapel

Henry III [1]
(1216–72)

[2] **Edward I** = *Eleanor of Castile* [3]
(1272–1307)

Edward II
(1307–27)

[4] **Edward III** = *Philipa of Hainault* [5]
(1327–77)

[6] *Edward the Black Prince*   *Joan de la Tour* [7]   *John of Gaunt Duke of Lancaster*   *Lionel* [8] *Duke of Clarence*   *Edmund* [9] *Duke of York*   *Mary* [10] *of Brittany*   *William* [11] *of Hatfield*

[12] **Richard II** = *Anne of Bohemia* [13]
(1377–99)

Henry IV
(1399–1413)

Richard Earl of Cambridge

[14] **Henry V** = *Catherine* [15]
(1413–22)   *of Valois* = *Owen Tudor*

Richard Duke of York

Henry VI
(1422–61)

[16]* *Margaret Beaufort* = *Edmund Tudor*

Edward IV = *Elizabeth Woodville*   **Richard III**
(1461–83)   *(1483–85)*

[17]* **Henry VII** = *Elizabeth* [18]*
(1485–1509)   *of York*

Edward V [19]*
(1483)

Richard [20]*
Duke of York

October 13th 1399
Coronation of Henry IV

March 20th 1413
Death of Henry IV in Jerusalem Chamber

April 9th 1413
Coronation of Henry V
Body of Richard II reburied at Westminster Abbey.

November 7th 1422
Funeral of Henry V

November 6th 1429
Coronation of Henry VI

1453
End of the Hundred Years War
The English finally swept out of Normandy and Aquitaine

June 28th 1461
Coronation of Edward IV

April 9th 1461
Prince Edward (later Edward V) born in Abbot's House

1477–91
Caxton printing in the Precinct

1483
Queen Elizabeth (Woodville) and son Prince Richard of York take sanctuary. Disappearance and probable murder of both Princes in the Tower

July 6th 1483
Coronation of Richard III

According to Pudlicott's subsequent confession, he began to excavate a tunnel from St Margaret's Churchyard through the 13-ft. thick foundation wall of the Chapter House, sowing hempseed to cover his activities. When winter turned to spring and the hemp flourished, he entered the Royal Wardrobe by night on April 24th, and remained there until April 26th, selecting his treasures. This confession is unconvincing, and was probably intended to protect his monastic accomplices, chiefly Adam of Warfield, who is likely to have handed the treasures to Pudlicott, who then passed them on to confederates for their removal both by land and water. A boatman curiously named Godde was implicated. There was no alarm until bits and pieces of booty began to be found. A fisherman netted a silver goblet; a woman of easy virtue received a precious ring from 'Dom Adam the Sacrist so that she should become his friend'; treasures were picked up in St Margaret's Churchyard.

The burglary of the Royal Treasury was recorded in a later cartoon in Matthew Paris's *Chronicles*.

At length rumours reached the king in Linlithgow; in June an inspection was ordered, and an inventory compiled of treasures lost and found. A search yielded more discoveries: under the beds of Skenche and William, in Pudlicott's lodging, with Adam the Sacrist, other monks and their servants. The whole convent was indicted and sent to the Tower of London, and judicial commissions sat to hear the case. In March 1304 William and five other lay suspects were hanged. Edward came south in triumph in 1305, released the monks, restored Skenche to his office, but had Pudlicott hanged in October 1305. He also transferred his chief Treasury to the Tower.

Contemporary accounts sought to minimize the monastic scandal, and it certainly seems now that the monks got off lightly, though Pudlicott was probably flayed as well as hanged. In a grotesque consequence over 500 years later, George Gilbert Scott, Surveyor of the Fabric, discovered 'a strange archaeological phenomenon—in an old wine cellar close to the Chapter House door from the Cloister—skin fastened to the door under the hinges, which has been proved to be human!' So Pudlicott's outer layer may have been pinned there as a warning to monks and others, rather as a gamekeeper hangs his moles and rooks on a fence. Scott's discovery also suggests that the Treasury may have been located in the Chapel of the Pyx, across the vestibule of the Chapter House from St Faith's Chapel, rather than in the crypt.

It is not surprising that Edward's last recorded use of the Abbey in 1306 should have been spectacularly offhand. In order to strengthen his Scottish expedition, he proclaimed throughout the land that all youths who were to become knights by inheritance and had the means to fight should present themselves at Westminster at the Feast of Pentecost, and the king would there supply them with all the accoutrements of knighthood (except a horse) from the obviously replenished royal wardrobe. The Prince of Wales led a great number into the Sacrarium of the Abbey, which was so crowded that some died in the crush and the Prince had to perform the ceremony standing on the high altar. A year later Edward I was dead, and at his son's coronation as Edward II, the Coronation Chair, designed to house the Stone of Scone beneath the oak seat of the English king, was first occupied. But it was an unsatisfactory proceeding. Piers Gaveston, Edward's friend and lover, chose to carry St Edward's crown, as well as taking charge of the entire mismanaged ceremonial, using it as an opportunity for self-display. 'None was neare to Piers in bravery of apparell or delicacie of fashion,' noted a chronicler. A severer tone prevailed in 1327, when the young Edward III was crowned twelve days after his father's deposition. 'Vox populi, vox dei', was the admonitory text of the Archbishop of Canterbury's sermon.

Fire, theft, and finally plague. Beneath a great black stone slab in the South Cloister lie nearly half the Benedictine brethren carried off by the Black Death in 1349, which also struck down Abbot Byrcheston.

Corbel in the North Transept thought to represent Henry's son, later Edward I.

Facing page: The Coronation Chair was built on the orders of Edward I in the first years of the 14th century to house the Stone of Destiny (Stone of Scone) which he had captured after defeating the Scots at the Battle of Dunbar in 1296. First used at the Coronation of his son Edward II in 1308, it has been the Coronation seat of twenty-eight monarchs. The Stone is now kept in Scotland (see p.142.)

The Pyx Chapel opens off the East Cloister. Its formidable door indicates that it was once a stronghold for the Royal Treasury. The 'pyx' was a box in which specimen gold and silver coins were held as a standard to test the purity of the coinage.

Though many figures of weepers (mourners) on medieval tombs have been stolen or mutilated, the ambulatory side of Edward III's tomb (*facing page*) still has entire gilt-bronze images of six of his fourteen children. The three above are Joan de la Tour, Lionel Duke of Clarence, and Edward the Black Prince.

In his place was elected one of the survivors, the young Simon Langham. A man of great ability and equally great ambition, he rose rapidly to be Treasurer of England, Bishop of Ely, Archbishop of Canterbury and, in 1368, a Cardinal at the Papal court at Avignon. Though Westminster was only a stepping-stone in his career, his love and care for it were unceasing, both during his life and at his death. His benefactions to the Abbey in his will came to more than £10,000. No one was more eager to see the rebuilding of the Nave resumed, and an exchange of letters with Nicholas Litlyngton, his successor as Abbot, in 1376, the last year of Langham's life, leaves no doubt about his wishes. Litlyngton writes, in April: 'You must know that since Michaelmas there have been seven masons continually at work and three at the quarry at Reigate, and since Christmas ten masons to pull down the side of the old church next the cloister. And all is in readiness now for rising twelve feet in height and three pillars in length. I myself laid the first stone on the first Monday in Lent in honour of God and St Peter, and in the name of our most honoured lord.' Langham's impatience is relayed through his secretary: 'It seems to him that, all things considered, the workmen are too slow at their work, half-hearted and slack.' Litlyngton is nettled and defensive, replying that money has to go for other things beside workmen: for stone, both from the quarry and else-

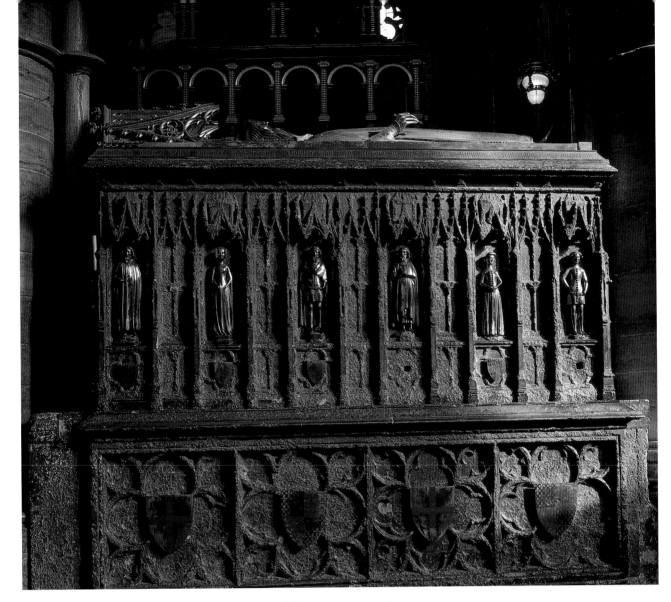

where, and for rubble. 'And besides, it would be easier to make a new church somewhere else than to pull down the old one there.'

Langham's bequest nudged the work forward. Richard II promised £100 a year from 1387, but his financial difficulties may have prevented regular payments. Purbeck marble pillars cost £40 each, and Langham had suggested that plain stone pillars would serve; Litlyngton insisted on Purbeck for the main pillars, but conceded Reigate stone, carted to Battersea and brought by boat to Westminster Mill, for the side aisles. All work stopped with Richard II's deposition in 1399. But at Henry V's Coronation, on Passion Sunday 1413, 'a ful trobly wet day, a sore ruggie and tempestuous day, with wind, snow and sleet', the new king felt both chill and shame at the semi-ruined state of the Nave. He assigned 1,000 marks a year from the Treasury for the work's continuation, and appointed Cardinal Beaufort and Richard Whittington, Surveyor of the Customs, hero of rags-to-riches folk tale and many a provincial pantomime, to supervise finances for the completion. But at Henry's death, the work was unfinished, stagnated for a further fifty years of civil strife, and lost royal support. Ostensibly, royal patronage was restored with the establishment of the Yorkist line by Edward IV in 1461, displacing the Lancastrian, but the new king's promise of money was seldom fulfilled: 'De dono domini

A Censing angel, one of four exquisitely carved 13th-century figures below the rose windows in the North and South Transepts.

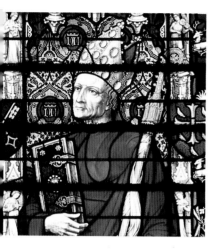

Abbot Litlyngton, here commemorated in an early 20th-century window, left as a gift to the Abbey the Missal completed in 1384 which was commissioned by him and carries his name. The book is still held in the Abbey Library.

Facing page: Christ Crucified: a full-page illumination from the Litlyngton Missal.

Below: From the same book, the coronation of a king, the arms of the monastery (left) and the three lions of England (right) in the borders.

Regis centum librarum—nihil hoc anno.' But Abbots Millyng and Esteney (1462–98) both set their energies to the enterprise. The junction with Henry III's building at the sixth bay west of the crossing, and the west window and roof above it were the final challenges. Esteney's 235 oaks costing £78 10s. 11d. and 31 fodders of lead costing £187 15s. 5d. were the last major expenditure on materials. By 1500, about 250 years after Henry III's church was begun, and about 125 years after Litlyngton laid the first stone of the new nave, the founder's vision was complete. The new work had cost £25,000 (£8.8m), of which £6000 had come from the crown: £1,685 from Richard II, £3,861 from Henry V, £519 from Edward IV. The surprising architectural conservatism which approved the copying of 13th-century French Gothic at the end of the 15th century and makes the nave of Westminster one of the earliest of all architectural fakes, was founded on intrinsic respect for the original structure, and consolidated by the snail's pace of progress. The design and scale of the Perpendicular west window apart, the visitor's eye is broadly seduced into an impression of unity. In this sense there is much to be thankful for in the retarding forces, political and financial, of the years between 1272 and 1500.

The election of Langham as Abbot in 1349 had restored fortune to Westminster after a half-century's absence. In 1344 Edward III and his elder son, the Black Prince, visited St Edward's Shrine before the French campaign crowned by victory at Poitiers, and presented the head of St Benedict as a relic. For the next hundred years, reigning monarchs in distress and facing military or political ordeals were accustomed to pray first at the shrine of the royal saint, a practice emphasising the personal and exclusive bond between a king and his idealised predecessor. Again before a journey abroad, in 1359, Edward III commended his affairs to St Edward and heard Mass. After the rituals he called his nobles around him and said: 'It is declared that I ought to be buried with the three Magi at Cologne; but most assuredly I do not intend them to be disquieted and moved for my sepulchre. See this present place, more worthy and more fair! The place too of my first honouring, wherein also most honourably rest Christ's well-beloved confessor Edward, once king of England, and his most devoted client Henry the king, and Edward the king, my noble grandsire. . . . who, I ask you, shall stay me from burial, according to my wish and my devotion, here in my own church, amid three illustrious kings?' '

The royal circle included Abbot Litlyngton, allegedly a bastard son of Edward III, whose tastes were elevated. His passion was falconry; his accounts include 2s. given to Henry Cophele to search for a missing hen-falcon, and 3s. 4d. to the king's falconer when he returned it, 6d. for a falcon of wax to be offered for a sick falcon, and 46s. 8d. to purchase a new bird (a

carthorse cost 66s. 8d.). But he did not neglect his responsibilities as abbot: he had the cloister completed as well as the most splendid of the 14th-century domestic buildings around the little square of the Abbot's Courtyard — College Hall, the Abbot's state dining-room, and the Jerusalem Chamber, his private dining-room, where his mitre and initials alternate on the painted oak roof with the crown and initials of Richard II. He was spirited, too; we have a glimpse of him as an old man buckling on his armour and sallying off to fight the French.

Richard II's devotion to the Confessor was at least as fervent as Henry III's. 'By St Edward' was his favourite oath, and the Wilton Diptych depicts the young king, wearing a gold and scarlet cloak embroidered with the white hart, his heraldic beast, under the special protection of a white-robed Confessor holding the gold ring which he had bestowed on the disguised beggar. Throughout his reign he treated the Abbey as a private fiefdom: the contemporary portrait of him that now hangs at the west end of the Nave, and the painted white hart in the gallery known as the Muniment Room in the South Transept were tokens of his proprietorial relation to Westminster.

His coronation on the July 16th 1377, when he was only 10 years old, is the first coronation of which we have a highly detailed account, in Thomas Walsingham's *Historia Anglicana*. The bishops and monks led Richard in procession from the Palace to the Abbey, singing an antiphon in honour of St Peter. At the altar he prostrated himself. He was led to his seat and a bishop preached a sermon on how a king should bear himself towards his people and how his people should obey him. Next he took the oath: to protect the Church, to uphold good laws and abrogate bad, and to judge rightly between men rather than show partiality. Lengthy blessings by the Archbishop followed. All this time, the Wardens of the Cinque Ports were holding over him a great silk canopy, bronze in colour, supported by a spear at each corner. During the anointing of his hands, head, chest, shoulders and arms, the choir sang the antiphon 'Zadok the priest and Nathan the prophet'. At the hymn 'Veni Creator Spiritus', he was raised by the Archbishop from his prostrate position and clothed in the tunic, dalmatic and stole of St Edward. A sword, bracelets and a pall were delivered to him. The Archbishop blessed the crown, and placed it on the king's head with a further blessing, before he was invested with ring, sceptre and verge. Then followed the benediction, the enthronement, and Mass. No wonder that the boy king, 'being opprest with fatigue and long fasting,' had to be carried from the Abbey to the Palace for the banquet on the shoulders of his tutor, Sir Simon Burley. In the jostling crowd one of the Confessor's slippers, part of the sacred regalia, fell from his foot and was lost. The Coronation Papers primly protest 'that at the coronation of King Richard in the eleventh year of his age many defects are found. Imprimis, one shoe, of the right foot, was lost by the negligence and defect of Sir Simon Burle, knight, who carried the said King on his shoulders from the church, contrary to ancient custom, the Abbot of the place protesting.' But a marble column topped by a gold eagle flowed with wine from all four sides for the whole Coronation

In the Jerusalem Chamber, the Abbot's State room, Nicholas Litlyngton's mitre and initials alternate on the painted oak ceiling with the crown and initials of Richard II.

Facing page: The left-hand panel of the Wilton Diptych showing Richard II with Edmund the Martyr, Edward the Confessor, and St John the Baptist

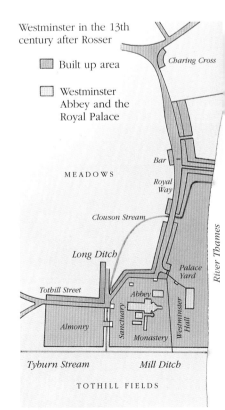

Westminster in the 13th century after Rosser

▨ Built up area

▢ Westminster Abbey and the Royal Palace

Charing Cross

MEADOWS

Bar

Royal Way

Clowson Stream

Long Ditch

River Thames

Tothill Street

Palace Yard

Abbey

Sanctuary

Westminster Hall

Almonry

Monastery

Tyburn Stream *Mill Ditch*

TOTHILL FIELDS

Richard II at his coronation: a portrait which has hung in the Abbey for more than 600 years.

Visiting Heads of State customarily visit the Abbey to lay a wreath on the Tomb of the Unknown Warrior. President Clinton did so in 1995, but the tradition of state visits goes back to Leo XI of Armenia in 1386.

Day, and all, even the very poorest of men, were allowed to drink from it. Who cared about a lost slipper?

Who in 1377 cared about Wat Tyler? But in 1381 he led the Peasants' Revolt, which presented the young king with a violent challenge. Lambeth was sacked, and Archbishop Sudbury dragged from the Tower and beheaded; Flemings were massacred, the Royal Treasury at Westminster attacked. The next day, June 15th, the mob returned to Westminster, where Richard Imworth, Steward of the Marshalsea Prison, had taken refuge and was clasping the columns at St Edward's Shrine. The rioters invaded the church, dragged him from the holy place and beheaded him. That same afternoon Richard visited the Abbey, 'to supplicate at the shrine of the sainted king for divine aid where human counsel was altogether wanting'. He heard Mass, and prayed before a statue of the Virgin, and 'every man, as he rose from prayer, took fresh heart, and fresh hope of a happy outcome!' The royal party then rode on to Smithfield, where they confronted the rebels and quelled the revolt.

In 1386 Richard entertained Leo XI of Armenia by leading him on a visit to the Abbey, anticipating by six hundred years the customary appearances now expected of visiting Heads of State; and in 1390 he joined the Feast of the Translation of St Edward, when he was present at vespers, compline, midnight matins, the procession and high mass. But the Abbey was defiled by the king himself in 1394. His beloved wife, Anne of Bohemia, from whose coronation the Abbey Library preserves a magnificent book, the *Liber Regalis*, had died of plague at Sheen Palace. The leading nobles had been summoned by an imperious letter to attend both the procession to Westminster and the funeral Mass on August 3rd. Froissart described the high drama of a night-time ritual with flambeaux and torches, an illumination greater than any that had ever been seen. The Earl of Arundel had been absent from the lying in state and procession, and pushed late into the proceedings in the Abbey, where he asked the king's leave to retire again immediately on urgent private affairs. Richard was so outraged by the insult that he seized a mace from a verger and struck Arundel, bleeding from the blow, to the floor. The churchmen suspended the service at this act of sacrilege which had polluted the sanctuary. The proud and turbulent Arundel became an implacable enemy, and joined the subsequent plots against the king, for which he was eventually sent to the scaffold.

As Richard's reign darkened towards his deposition in 1399 by Henry Bolingbroke, the monks were understandably fearful that the change of dynasty would sever their privileged royal favour. In December 1399, Abbot Colchester was at the centre of a plot laid in his house to murder Henry IV and his sons at Windsor. 'Come home with me to supper, I will lay/ A plot shall show us all a merry day' The Abbot of Westminster in Shakespeare's *Richard II* thus invites

From the *Liber Regalis*, a service book perhaps prepared for the coronation of Anne of Bohemia, wife of Richard II in 1382.

Left: Coronation of a queen.

Below:
Detail from coronation of a king.

Aumerle and the Bishop of Carlisle to be his accomplices. But Aumerle, noted double-dealer, betrayed him and Colchester was arrested and sent to the Tower. 'Certyn monks of Westr' were also put in prison in Ludgate, but all were later released. Ironically, it was in Colchester's house that Henry IV was to die in 1413.

It had become the custom, before a coronation, for the new king to reside for a week in the Tower, and then, on the day before his coronation, process in a cavalcade cum pageant through London to Westminster. Henry IV had chosen October 13th, which was also St Edward's Day, because it was the anniversary of the day on which Richard had sent him into exile. On October 11th, there is the first record of the creation of knights of the Order of the Bath, who were to accompany him through the city. Forty-six knights, including three of the king's sons, bathed together at the Tower in a ritual of purification irreverently reminiscent of a rugby club changing-room. It seems that Henry did not himself take part, for at the coronation his head was observed to be swarming with lice, an event regarded as ill-omened. One of the beneficiaries of Coronation Day, was Geoffrey Chaucer, who was granted an annuity of 40 marks 'for good service

Geoffrey Chaucer, civil servant, was buried in the Abbey in 1400. The tomb to Chaucer as author of *The Canterbury Tales* was erected in the 16th century, and became the nucleus of the future Poets' Corner.

Henry IV's coronation in 1399. The future Henry V, in black armour, stands among the group to the left of the 'pulpitum' — the raised platform used for coronations and funerals.

rendered to the new king'. As Collector of Customs and Clerk of Works to the Palace of Westminster he had proved a good public servant, and had enjoyed the patronage of John of Gaunt. He was also granted the lease of a house in the Abbey precincts, on the north side of the Lady Chapel, and may have been placed there by Henry as a spy, to keep watch on the disaffected Abbot and monks. If so, his usefulness was short-lived, for he died there in 1400. His burial in the south transept of the Abbey was the seed of the future Poets' Corner, but at the time the motivation was political rather than literary.

The death of Henry IV in the Abbot's House on St Cuthbert's Day, March 20th 1413, and the accession of Prince Hal as Henry V after the episode of taking the crown from his father's deathbed, is part of the folklore of English history, thanks in large measure to Shakespeare's extended dramatic treatment of it in *King Henry IV, Part II*. Robert Fabyan's contemporary chronicle strips the event of its literary and historical accretions. The king was saying prayers at St Edward's shrine, to take his leave and to seek grace to speed him on his journey to the Holy Land, where he intended to visit the Holy Sepulchre. But all of a sudden he was 'so suddenlie and greevouslie taken sick, that such as were about him feared that he would have died right there. Wherefore they, for his comfort, bore him into the Abbot's place and lodged him in a chamber, and there upon a pallet laid him before the fire, where he lay in great agony a certain of time.' Coming to himself, he asked where he was, and whether the chamber had a name. Told that it was called Jerusalem, he said, 'Loving be to the Father of Heaven, for now I know I shall die in this chamber, according to the prophecy of me beforehand, that I should die in Jerusalem.' Being thought dead, his face was covered with a linen cloth, and Prince Henry took the crown away. His father regained consciousness and missed the crown. Henry was summoned back. Here Fabyan records the nub of an exchange that Shakespeare was to seize on:

'Sir, to mine and all men's judgements you seemed dead in this world, so I as your next heir apparent took that as mine owne, and

not as yours.' 'Well, faire sonne,' said the king (with a great sigh), 'what right I had to it, God knoweth.' 'Well,' said the prince, 'if you die King, I will have the garland, and trust to keepe it with the sword against all mine enemies, as you have done.' Then said the king, 'I commit all to God, and remember you to do well. With that he turned himself in his bed, and shortlie after departed to God.'

It seems that, in the place and circumstances of his father's death, Henry V sensed a curse lurking. Not only did he show prompt enthusiasm to finish the rebuilding of the nave, but he also brought the coffin of Richard II back from King's Langley in an act of penitence and reparation, to lie beside Anne of Bohemia, even using the banners that had been part of his father's funeral rites at Canterbury. In the night before the Battle of Agincourt, in Shakespeare's *Henry V*, the king prays, 'O Lord!/ O! not today, think not upon the fault/ My father: made in compassing the crown./ I Richard's body have interred anew,/ And on it have bestow'd more contrite tears/ Than from it issu'd forced drops of blood.'

The Lord heard; Agincourt was won. When the news reached London, all the bells were rung, and all the religious orders joined a procession from St Paul's to St Edward's shrine at Westminster. The victory was celebrated by the first recorded service of thanksgiving in the Abbey on November 23rd 1415, which the king attended not in magnificence but in simple dress. He refused to display to the people his helmet scarred in battle, but popular imagination later invested the tournament helmet that hung on a beam above his tomb with Agincourt magic, though it had only been supplied for the effigy at his funeral.

The first scene of Shakespeare's *Henry VI, Part I* is set in the Abbey, at Henry's funeral seven years later in 1422. 'Hung be the heavens with black, yield day to night,' laments Bedford. Henry V had died of dysentery at Vincennes at midnight on August 31st, at the end of an excessively hot summer of campaigning in France. The grief that attended his death was the spur to one of the most sumptuous funerals the Abbey has seen. A long procession brought the body from Paris to Calais, and from Dover to London, on which stage of the journey four intermediate funerals were celebrated. There were further obsequies at St Paul's before the cortège reached the Abbey. Here the royal standards of France and England were carried for the first and only time at a royal funeral, as a chariot containing the embalmed body of the king in a lead coffin, accompanied by torches and white robed priests, was drawn by four horses up the nave as far as the quire. Behind that his three chargers were led up to the altar steps. The hearse in the presbytery was surrounded by sixty poor men with wax torches. He had been as bold in planning his funeral as on the field at Agincourt. His will was detailed and peremptory: the relics at the east end of St Edward's Chapel, containing the shrine, were to be rehoused, and a high chantry chapel raised over his tomb, where 20,000 Masses were to be said for his soul. Here he was buried, 'with suche solempne ceremonies, suche mounyng of lordes, suche prayer of pryestes, such

Henry V ordered that the body of Richard II, deposed by his father Henry IV, should be brought to the Abbey from King's Langley for burial: 'I Richard's body have interred anew.'

lamentynge of commons as never was before that daye sene in the
Realme of Englande.' His tomb was popularly regarded as that of a
saint, and the stone steps to it worn by the feet and knees of monks
and visitors indicate that it became a far more magnetic place of
pilgrimage than the Confessor's shrine had ever been.

A more vulgar popularity was to be the lot of his widow,
Katherine de Valois, who after Henry's death married a Welshman
called Owen Tudor and was thus the unwitting founder of a later
dynasty. She died in 1437, and was buried in the Lady Chapel, but
was taken up in 1503 when work on the new chapel was begun by
Henry VII. The dispossessed queen was callously left unburied, in a
coffin of boards, behind the east end of the quire. Here she was
displayed by the 'tomb-shewers' to such visitors as Pepys, who in his
diary for 1669 lubriciously records a visit to Westminster to see the
tombs. 'Queen Katherine of Valois. Had her upper part of her body
in my hands. And I did kiss her mouth, reflecting upon it that I did
kiss a Queen, and that this was my birthday, 36 year old, that I did
first kiss a Queen.' It was two hundred years more before Dean
Stanley took pity on her wandering and abused remains, and had
them buried in the chapel of Henry V's Chantry.

In 1422 her infant son had succeeded his father as Henry VI
at the age of nine months. The Coronation Regalia did
not include nappies, and the ceremony was postponed
until his eighth year, 1429. Both the solemn wonder and
the endearing playfulness of the bewildered child are
suggested in a contemporary account: 'And he was set
in his astate in the myddes of the scaffold there, behold-
ynge the people all abowte sadly and wysely. [At the
shrine] he was arayed as a kynge in riche cloth of gold,
with a crowne on his hede; which crowne the kyng dyd
doo make for hym self.' Like Henry III and Richard II,
also crowned as boy kings, Henry VI grew up devoted
to the Abbey and St Edward's shrine. He revived the
older custom of naming his firstborn son Edward. As the
Wars of the Roses submerged his reign in blood and disorder, his habit was to visit the Abbey at all hours to seek
solace and to choose his own place of burial. On one
occasion, he visited the Confessor's Chapel with Abbot
Kirton and John Flete, the Prior, praying at his father's
tomb, and then from the Chantry above surveying the
chapel for more than an hour. It was proposed to move
Henry V's tomb to one side so that his son could be
alongside him. 'Nay, let him alone; he lieth like a noble
prince. I would not trouble him.' At last he turned his
attention to the space between the shrine and the tomb
of Henry III, and marked with his foot seven feet. 'Here
methinketh is a convenient place. Forsooth, forsooth,
here will we be! Here is a good place of us!' John
Thirske, master mason, took an iron pick, and traced the
length of the grave on the pavement. A long wavering

Facing page: The Chantry Chapel
to the east of the Confessor's
shrine was built to house the
tomb of Henry V who died on
campaign in France in 1422.
The Chapel is in the form of
both a capital 'H' and a medieval
gatehouse. The rich statuary
depicts Henry as king of both
England and France.

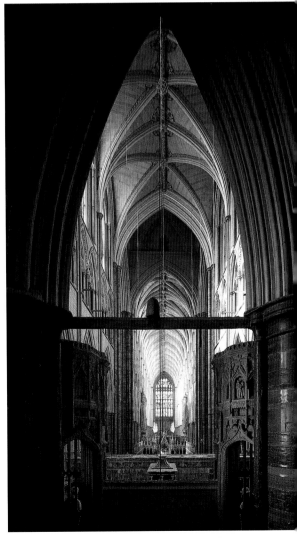

Henry VI's view westwards from
his father's Chantry Chapel (see
foot of page)

scratch identified with antiquarian delight 460 years later by Francis Westlake and Lawrence Tanner, who had persuaded the innocent Dean Ryle to order the temporary removal of the linoleum covering the floor of the chapel, 'because it was unsuitable for the Installation of Knights of the Bath', without divulging their real purpose. But Henry never lay in his chosen place: he died by violence, and was quietly buried at Chertsey Abbey.

Violence engulfed Yorkists as well as Lancastrians as the dynastic struggle rolled on. Elizabeth Woodville, queen to Edward IV, had given birth to his eldest son, Edward, while claiming sanctuary in the Abbot's house in 1470. After her husband's death she returned there in 1483, with five daughters and her second son, Richard Duke of York, aged 9. Richard of Gloucester, Shakespeare's most celebrated villain, whom she was fleeing, had his own eye on the Crown. He persuaded the Archbishop of Canterbury to use his influence with the Queen. With many misgivings, she was persuaded to give up her son. There was a scene of pitiful parting: 'Farewell, mine own sweet son, God send you good keeping: let me kiss you yet once, ere you go; for God knoweth when wee shall kisse together againe. And therewithall she kissed him, and blessed him, turned her back and wept, and went on her way, leaving the child weeping as fast'.

Henry VI was crowned in the Abbey in 1429 when he was a boy of 9. Though he expressed a wish for a tomb there, he was buried quietly at Chertsey Abbey after his murder in the Tower of London in 1471.

The bones of two boys were discovered in The Tower of London in 1674, and were reburied in the Abbey at the command of Charles II, in the belief that they were the remains of the Princes in the Tower, Edward V and his younger brother Richard. A scientific examination in 1933 did not disprove the story. This is the skull of the older boy.

In June 1483 Richard was taken to the Tower to join his elder brother, and though observers glimpsed them playing together in July, they were soon seen no more, and were probably murdered in August. It was given out that they had died of fever, and the news was brought to their mother at Westminster. 'It stroke her harte like the sharp darte of death . . . she swooned and fell to the ground and there lay in great agony, like a dead corpse. Her breast she punched, her fair hair she tore and pulled in pieces . . . after long lamentations, she kneeled down and cried to God to take vengeance.'

In 1674 the bones of two boys were found at the foot of a staircase in the Tower, and were buried by order of Charles II in the monument designed by Wren in the south aisle of the Lady Chapel. In 1933 the urn was opened, and the remains studied. The age and relationship of the boys, and the violent manner of their deaths, together with the site of their grave in the Tower, are not incompatible with the supposition that has captured the public imagination. The story had a pathetic epilogue in 1964. Richard of York, at the age of 4, had been married to the 5-year-old Anne Mowbray, on January 15th 1477/8, in St Stephen's Chapel in the Palace of

Westminster. She died in 1481, and was buried in the Chapel of St Erasmus, built and endowed at the south-east corner of the Abbey by Elizabeth Woodville. This chapel was prematurely demolished in 1502 to make room for Henry VII's Lady Chapel. She was disinterred, and reburied, according to the antiquary William Camden, in the Chapel of our Lady of the Pew, renamed St Erasmus' Chapel by Abbot Islip at the time of the demolition. But in 1964 her lead coffin was found on the site of the Church of Minoresses of St Clare, in Stepney. Her coffin plate read 'Hic jacet Anna ducissa Ebor filia et heres Johannis ducis Norff'. And in May 1965 she was reburied in the Lady Chapel, next to her original burial place, and within easy haunting distance of her young husband.

Times of great political disorder are often creative in unexpected ways. After early years spent in Cologne and Bruges, William Caxton had settled in Westminster in 1476, in a large house called St Albans on the south side of the Lady Chapel, and a shop was let to him for 10s. per annum. Westminster was a good place for a printing business, for between St Albans and the Abbey, a path led from old Palace Yard to the door into the south transept used by members of the Commons on their way to meetings in the Chapter House. He paid his rent for this shop or booth every year until his death. Later, in 1482, he took additional premises in the Abbey Almonry known as The Red Pale, probably a personal trade mark hung outside. It was here that he died in 1491 or 1492. But by then had appeared a succession of books 'emprynted by me William Caxton in the abbey of Westminster': the *Canterbury Tales* (1477), the *History of Jason and Boethius* (1478) among them. Wynkyn de Worde, Caxton's assistant and successor, continued to pay rent for the old shop until 1500, when he moved to Fleet Street.

Acute political instability coincided with forces that were to drive Western Europe into cultural regeneration. Cardinal Bouchier officiated at three successive 'new dynasty' coronations in 14 years between 1471 and 1485: of Edward IV, Richard III and Henry VII. At the second of these, in 1483, though Richard and his queen went barefoot from Palace to Abbey, the monks were not deceived by his show of humility, and sang Te Deum 'with a faint courage'. The rumours surrounding the disappearance of Edward and Richard of York were in circulation, and their young lives had mingled with Westminster's in many ways, as the account of sanctuary in the next chapter is to show. But as the forces for change gathered, the life of the Benedictine Abbey was to enjoy a notable final flourishing before its extinction.

The urn, at the east end of the North Aisle of Henry VII's Chapel, designed by Sir Christopher Wren, which contains the bones of the two boys found in the Tower.

A monastic account book showing the payment of William Caxton's rent for his house and printing workshop.

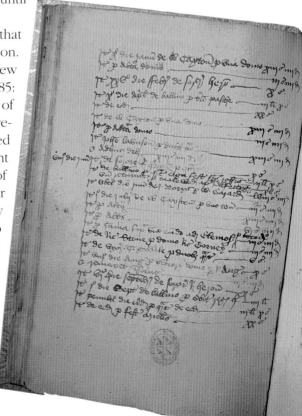

Medieval heads found beneath the monk's refectory.

'Black' monks from the Litlyngton Missal.

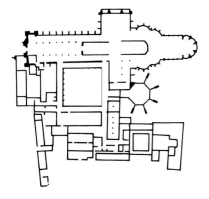

The monastic precinct.

Abbot Byrcheston and 26 monks died when the Black Death swept through Europe in 1348 and 1349. A huge black slab in the South Cloister is supposed to mark their common tomb.

Life in the Monastery

In counterpoint to the stir and fret created by royalty and acts of God, the disproportioning of the sensational, as in our urgent news bulletins, were the days, decades and centuries of monastic routine. Here were found the comforting continuities with which institutions recognise themselves — except, of course, where self-interest wheedled change in by the back door and, with ingenious argument, squared it with custom. The structure of habit holds the flabby wills of human agents approximately in place.

For 600 years the Benedictine ideal was pursued by the black robed monks at Westminster. This ideal was familial. With the Abbot as father, the brethren sought to lead a common and as far as possible self-sufficient life, observing strictly the round of the eight daily offices in the church, eating together in the refectory, sleeping in a common dormitory, meeting together each morning in the Chapter House, where a portion of the Benedictine rule was read daily to the community, participating in the daily Conventual Mass and saying Masses for the dead. Additionally, in the north cloister which caught the best of the day's warmth they read and copied manuscripts and wrote chronicles and the lives of saints.

Abbot Ware's 'Customary' of 1266–72, closely modelled on that written by Lanfranc for the monks at Canterbury, provides a long and detailed account of the Benedictine round. In the choir of Henry III's church there were sixty-two stalls, matching a community of fifty-five to sixty monks in the thirteenth century. It had been larger—Abbot Crispin (c. 1100) had set aside revenues sufficient to clothe eighty monks—and was to be smaller: only twenty-nine in 1353–4 after the Black Death. After that forty-eight seems to have been the optimum number: forty priests and eight novices. But by the 1490s, the community had grown to fifty-nine, the highest figure formally recorded. In addition there were about 100 servants, often holding hereditary office. Novices, drawn from London and the estates owned by the Abbey in the provinces, generally entered the monastery between the ages of 18 and 20, often after attending the Almonry School or Song School. Their Christian names were unvarying: John, William, Thomas, Richard, Robert, Henry were shared by two-thirds of the 700 monks of whom we have record; their surnames were frequently place names: Pershore, Reading, Aldenham, Sudbury, Colchester. Gifts in kind ('exennia') marked the two milestones in a monk's career: his first Mass, after which he received bread and wine to make merry, and his promotion 'ad skillam' (at the bell) to the senior table in the refectory, which qualified him to preside over a meal.

The monastic day was, like ours, divided into 24 hours but before the invention of mechanical clocks in the 13th century, the 12 hours of the night were shorter than the 12 hours of the day. The hours also varied between summer and winter. In winter the day ran from about 2 a.m. to 7 p.m. The round of services began with Matins, followed by Lauds before dawn, and Prime at 7 a.m. Then there was private reading and washing. Terce was at 9 a.m., leading to Chapter meeting and a spell of physical work until 12.30 p.m. Sext and Nones preceded dinner, the main meal of the day, at 2 p.m. Further reading before Vespers, then the evening meal and a drink in the Refectory, a public reading in the choir, Compline, the last office of the day around 7 p.m., after which the monks retired to bed for warmth as well as for rest. In the later Middle Ages hours became regularised. Matins would then be sung at midnight, and the brethren would return to bed until Lauds.

Despite the demands of the 'horarium', the monks did not lead a self-contained existence. Not only did Westminster's site and royal connections bring in many public figures to the meetings of the Great

c. 960
Foundation of Benedictine monastery by St Dunstan

c. 1070–1200 Laying out of the present precinct

1266–72 Abbot Ware's 'Customary' defines the order of monastic life

1303
Robbery in the Royal Treasury

1348–9
Black Death kills about half the monks, including the Abbot

1354 29 monks: lowest figure recorded

1370–80 Completion of the Abbot's House, College Hall, Jerusalem Chamber

1490–2 59 monks: highest figure recorded

1500 John Islip *Abbot*

1536 Seizure of land and treasure by Thomas Cromwell for Henry VIII

1540 Surrender of the Abbey to the king

A modern reconstruction of Thorney Island as it may have appeared in the 16th century, in the last years of the monastery.

The Abbey Library, with a 15th-century roof and 17th-century bookcases, was the north end of the monks' dormitory.

Facing page: 13th-century wall painting in St Faith's Chapel, perhaps 'Master William, the king's beloved painter', who was employed at the time in embellishing the Abbey.

The ornate 14th-century Doorway to the Refectory. Behind it now is the practice room for the Abbey Choir.

Council and Parliament in the Refectory and Chapter House, but monks received family visitors and travellers, especially from other Benedictine houses, and went to and fro freely into Westminster, or to Oxford for further study, or on holidays or pilgrimages. An initiated monk received wages; in 1500 a junior monk received £8 a year, a senior £12 (about £2,800 and £4,000 in modern terms). Necessarily, Benedictine life at Westminster imitated much of what it saw outside the walls, and progressively the ideal of disciplined common life was undermined as greater comforts in buildings, furnishings and food insinuated themselves. The common dormitory, with its straw beds on which a mattress or pallet was laid, proved specially unpopular, despite the introduction of curtained cubicles in the 14th century, and it was a regular practice for monastic officers to withdraw into their own private quarters, leaving scarcely half of the community to the trials of the dormitory. Night garments were introduced only at the end of the 15th century, and with baths occurring only four times a year, when a bath attendant was specially employed, dormitory life must have been offensive to most of the senses. The drift towards private life and secular activity was inexorable. In 1447 a brothel called the Maydenshed was alleged to be frequented by the monks; in 1462 archery butts were set up for them in the Infirmary Garden. Archery, at least, could be justified on the grounds of keeping them fit. Well before the ending of the monastery in 1540, the pattern of a less rigorous collegiate establishment was already in preparation, and it is an index of the ease of transition from Roman Catholic to Anglican, which simple history has disposed us to see as a watershed, that when Abbot Boston became the Dean of the new 'cathedral' which the Abbey briefly became, ten monks out of twenty-four on the roll also became either minor canons or prebendaries in the new order.

From the 10th century the Abbey was a substantial land-owner; from the 1060s it was a mighty one, encompassing not only tracts of land in the South-East, but also estates in the West Midlands that had once formed part of the endowments of Pershore Abbey and Deerhurst Priory. Rental income from the estates was its most important source of revenue. The Saxon manor of Eia, stretching from Westminster to Chelsea, which was later divided into Hyde, Neyte (now Victoria and Pimlico) and Ebury, was an early land endowment, and remained in monastic hands until conveyed to (i.e. taken by) Henry VIII, together with Convent Garden (later Covent Garden), in 1536. Other manors acquired were Hendon, Hampstead, Wandsworth and Belsize. In the 12th and 13th centuries, smaller plots of land were given as endowments in return for the prayers of the monks ('post-obit' prayers), a practice that largely ended at the time of Henry III's rebuilding. But from that time substantial revenues also accrued from the royal and aristocratic legacies intended to finance commemoration of the anniversaries of their deaths in perpetuity. Queen Eleanor's 'Manors' yielded far higher income than was necessary to meet the cost of these rituals. In 1390, 100 years after her death, it amounted to £300 8s. 4½ d., of which £6 12s. 6d. was spent on 250 lbs of wax, and £16 12s. 5d. on a distribution of 'dole' to the

Bronze tomb effigy of Eleanor of Castile, wife of Edward I, in St Edward's Chapel. For over 200 years the anniversary of her death was an occasion for the distribution of 'dole' by the Almonry to thousands of the poor.

Black robed Benedictine monks, from the Litlyngton Missal

poor. But a dividend of £150 10s. was paid as monks' wages, from the late 13th century onward, from the surplus revenues of foundations associated with royal anniversaries, principally those for Henry III, Eleanor of Castile, Richard II, Henry V, and, towards the end of the monastic period, Henry VII and Lady Margaret Beaufort. Lady Margaret's will required the distribution of 32,000 pence to the poor on the anniversaries of both her death day and her burial day. Gradually between 1300 and 1500, more and more revenue from the royal foundations was appropriated as 'wages' and less and less distributed to the poor. One rationale for this practice, not unheard in the days of the Welfate State, was an anxiety that indiscriminate alms-giving encouraged the idle beggar.

Funerals and coronations were lucrative events for the community. The sacrist and his assistants received handsome 'guerdons', and had the right to sell the trappings used in the ceremonies, even down to the hearses displaying the effigies at royal funerals. Waste wax from candles and torches burned at funerals, often several hundred pounds in weight, was gathered up and sold. Yet another source of income was provided by Henry III, who granted to the Abbot the right to hold two sixteen-day fairs each year, on January 5th, the day of the Confessor's death, and October 13th, the feast of his translation. All other trade within range of St Margaret's Churchyard, where it was first held, was prohibited. In 1298 the two fairs were ordered to combine into a single thirty-two-day fair, and to move to Tothill Fields, the watery meadows along the river to the south of the Abbey, once part of Bulinga fen. Visitors would combine the fair with a pilgrimage, though it seems St Edward's was never a widely popular cult. Receipts at their height in 1358–9 amounted to £74 offered at the shrine and reliquary.

From time to time, of course, substantial expenditure on the buildings was required, especially after the fire of 1298, when the infirmary, its chapel of St Catherine, the cloister and refectory all had to be repaired, and again in 1374 when the monks felt compelled to build the present precinct wall to defend themselves against such royal encroachment as Edward III's Jewel Tower of 1370. Even so, on balance, income far exceeded essential expenditure, and at the dissolution in 1540, Westminster was second only to Glastonbury in wealth, with an annual income of nearly £4,000.

It is from the accounts of the monastic officers that we can sense the textures of daily life. The Cellarer was the monastic housekeeper, presiding over his own range of buildings, between the monastic farm, granary, mill and brewhouse, and the kitchens. He employed as assistants a brewer and baker, a swineherd, winnower, miller, carter, stablehand, cooper, janitor and parlour servant. He was to see that there was no lack of cheese, wheat, barley, oats, wood and other necessaries. To him the monks applied in case of need. 'If anyone ask aught of him, let him grant it cheerfully if he can. If he cannot do so, let him refuse it kindly that the petitioner be not vexed,' is Abbot Ware's advice to the ideal cellarer. He was responsible, too, for hospitality: all visitors were given a loaf and flagon of beer. The Chamberlain's duty was to provide clothes, and his books record the annual buying in of black serge for habits, kersey for stockings and gaiters, linen for underclothing and shirts, and blanket to make slippers. In 1326–7 he buys twenty-three skins for winter boots, and 300 faggots of wood to heat the quarterly bath water for 10s.

The Almoner was the agent of monastic charity to the needy of the neighbourhood, and the Almonry building stood near the bridge and gatehouse to the west, facing the warren of little streets making up the village of Westminster, dominated by butchers and brothels. Of the indigent and sick of the locality, some lived in the Almonry, others received regular 'doles' in the form of soup or other basic foods. To be 'on the dole' and to be fed from 'a soup-kitchen',

Burial of a king, perhaps Edward III, from the Litlyngton Missal. Funerals and coronations were lucrative events for the community: not only were the monks entitled to the trappings, but also a royal bequest for Masses or alms distribution would swell revenue.

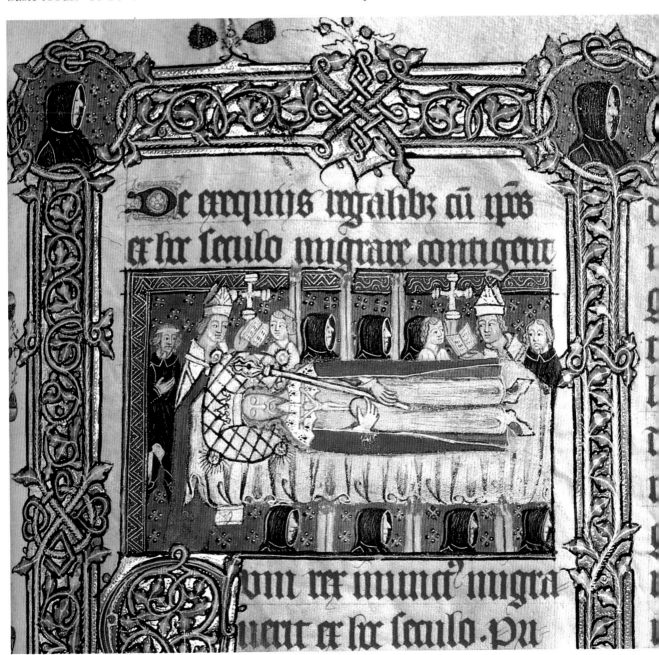

The Almonry also housed the Song School. Musical notation from the Litlyngton Missal.

Facing page:
An illustration from the prayer book of Lady Margaret Beaufort, mother of Henry VII, and one of the Abbey's greatest benefactors.

those 20th-century markers of social deprivation, are rooted in monastic charity. The dole-house, also known as 'the sope-house', was the popular name for the Almonry. Here Sir Thomas More observed the crowds, in such numbers 'that myself for the preace of them have ben fayne to ryde another waye. As farre as ever I harde, the munkes use not to sende awaye many unserved.' The daily practice in the Refectory of putting out the portion of food for a deceased monk for a year after his death, together with the setting aside of three or four rations of food in commemoration of the Maundy, all to be given to the poor, was a regular ritual, though the distribution of food seems to have shrunk to token gestures by comparison with the scale of alms distributions on royal anniversaries, funded by royal benefactions. On the best endowed of these, commemorating Eleanor of Castile and Lady Margaret Beaufort, up to 20,000 poor received alms in cash rather than kind. Since the population of Westminster up to 1540 did not exceed 3,000, compared with London's 35,000, such distributions must have attracted folk from far afield. The Almonry also housed the Song School and, from at least 1341, a school for poor local children which was to grow, over 600 years, into a school for rich cosmopolitan ones: Westminster School. The Almoner's accounts in the early 14th century include 60 lbs of peas and beans allotted to the poor during Lent, 15*d.* for the burial of two poor people, 5*s.* for two poor scholars setting off for Oxford, ½ lb. of wheat to Agnes Moode, a poor parishioner, and, in 1319, 13*s.* 8*d.* 'to keep little Nigel at school for a whole year for the love of God'.

Every great church, no doubt, attracted to its skirts a proportion of the poor, outcast and lawless. The regular distribution of alms brought in one swathe, the liberty of Westminster another. No doubt, too, that for centuries the labyrinths of little alleys encircling the Abbey were far more squalid than picturesque. But the ecclesiastical authorities who clung to the privilege of sanctuary ensured that Westminster was a sump of vice and crime. Their motives were not so much disinterested concern for the rights of sinners as the health of their accounts: in the 16th century the Abbey was eager to preserve the privilege of sanctuary because it raised the rental values of precinct houses. The meanness and squalor of the surrounding streets also sprang from the Abbey's refusal, like many a subsequent greedy and benighted landlord, either to sell land or grant long leases to tenants. The socially marginalised figures, the homeless, the winos, the bag ladies and the deranged who are still drawn to the

Glorious ihu. O mekest ihu. O most swe test ihu. I pray the that j may haue dene con

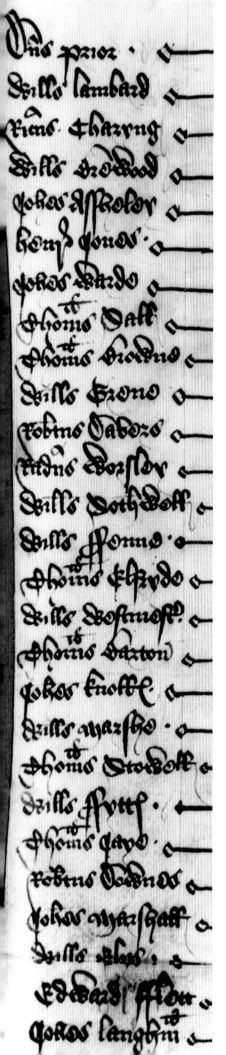

streets of Westminster around the Abbey, are, in their apparent dislocation from the present order, enacting their part in a past one.

Miss Barbara Harvey's lifetime of research in the Abbey records has opened the doors of Refectory and Infirmary, and beckoned us in to share the monastic diet and to follow its consequences to the place of sickness and medication. The two main meals of the day were dinner, around 11 a.m., and supper at about 6 p.m. The monks dined off pewter dishes, and were served in 'messes' of four. Bread, fish or meat, cheese, eggs, and ale comprised virtually their entire diet, though no meat was eaten in Lent or Advent, and no dairy produce in Lent. In theory there were four meat days a week, and three fish days, but the love of meat was such that a distinction was made between the misericord and the Refectory, two separate dining rooms. The original purpose of the misericord was to provide nourishing fare for monks who had been bled, or who had been sick. Fresh meat was served there on 150 days in the year, and as long as there was a quorum eating in the Refectory, the rules were felt to have been observed. Much casuistry was devoted to making a distinction between 'meat' and 'meaty dishes', which did not count as meat. Umble pie—entrails or offal cooked in ale—was judged a 'meaty dish', rather as a modern sausage or haggis might be. Favourite meats were mutton, beef, pork and veal, in that order; the Abbey had its own pig farm, garden (Covent Garden), orchard and vineyard. Each brother was allotted a daily loaf, weighing about 2 lbs; in 1402 John Longyng, baker, made 40,880 loaves. Fish was both preserved (salted, dried, pickled) and fresh: cod and whiting on ordinary days, conger eel, pike and salmon on feast days. In 1338 there is a record of payment of 2 pence to fishermen who brought 'St Peter's salmon' to the monastery. The Abbey malthouse brewed beer: the allowance was one gallon a day for each monk. It must indeed have been 'small beer'. The monks were especially fond of cheese flan and a pudding called dowcet, a custard of sugar, currants, cream and eggs. And for fifty-six glorious days a year, from Easter Day to Trinity Sunday, there were pancakes: 'Expenses laid out in respect of the pancakes prescribed for the brethren and delivered to the monastery according to custom, in the 12th year of the reign of King Richard II.'

Milk	126 gallons	@ 1d. the gallon	10s. 6d.
Butter	3 gallons, 3 qrts	@ 2s. 4d. the gallon	9s. 4d.
Eggs	5,816 eggs	@ 10d. the hundred	£2 8s 5d.
Salt	One peck	@ 3d.	

It is no surprise, given the levels of unrelieved protein in such a diet, that the Infirmary was a busy place. Permission to go there had to be sought at the daily chapter meeting. The common diseases of the monastic life were, predictably, liver complaints, obesity, and afflictions of the shin bone probably caused by vitamin C deficiency, excess weight, and poor circulation, perhaps the result of long hours of standing to sing offices. The Infirmarer's accounts show the commonest medicines purchased to have been honey for syrups, licorice, ginger, camomile, poppy, supplemented by herbs grown in the Infirmary garden. The engaging nicknames 'Dr Leech' and 'Dr Pill' also occur in the account books. In the Infirmary too the aged and 'infirm' were cared for, occupying their own cells and receiving pensions for their former services: the Abbey's own sheltered housing.

From such banalities of everyday life the Abbots of Westminster were often tempted. With great resources at his command, an abbot slipped easily into the role of political grandee, on terms with the greatest in the land, and residing at one of his own manors. Abbot Colchester's manors' stock in 1400 included 58 horses, 19 fowls, 351 head of cattle, 299 pigs, and 2,287 sheep and lambs. Abbots held, *ex officio*, important positions in court and politics, were customarily summoned to parliaments, and were backed by wealth enough to enable them to lead lavish lives in their own manorial estates. They had the use of up to a dozen houses, but the most frequented were Neyte, Hampstead, and Pyrford, in Surrey. Only on a handful of days a year did an abbot dine in the refectory with his brethren. In the middle of the 15th century, two successive abbots appear to have violated the proprieties to an unusual degree, or else aroused a unusual degree of envy. Abbot Kirton (1440–62) had pledged some of the Abbey plate and his own pastoral staff in the course of burdening the monastery with a huge debt. He was examined by papal mandate on charges of being a fornicator, a dilapidator, an adulterer and a simoniac, and was suspended, but contrived to make a comeback and be granted a generous pension. His successor, George Norwych, who as a young monk in 1447, had managed to set fire to the dormitory, 'about 9 at night, on the feast of Saints Crispin and Crispinian' — October 25th —, pursued his reckless career when he became Abbot. Four years of extravagant life with lavish hospitality accumulated debts under the seal of the convent of over £2,000, and the monks petitioned Henry VI for his suspension, beseeching him 'to consider the gret wast and destruccion of your seid monasterie and the grete mischief that it standeth in, and the hevy disclaudre that is reised and dayly encreceth upon your seid oratours thurgh the mysgovernaunce of their Abbot wheryn he dayly centynueth the weche withoute hasty remedie thurgh your grace provided will cause your seid monasterie to be utterly distroyed and under for evermore.' Norwych prudently retired from office.

College Garden, in the south-east corner of the precinct, was both an infirmary garden where medicinal herbs were grown, and the site of monastic fishponds and archery butts.

Facing page:
List of monks 1507–8.

A black-cowled Benedictine monk decorates a corner of the Litlyngton Missal.

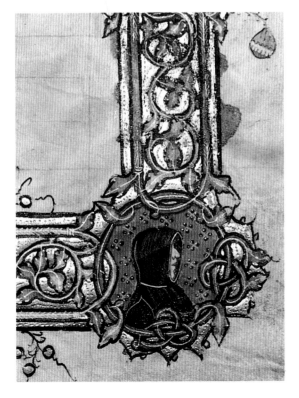

The Lady Chapel built by Henry VII.

Heraldic beasts in Henry VII's Chapel.

Indian Summer

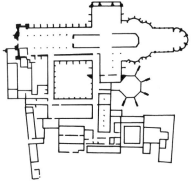

Henry VII's Lady Chapel (Blue).

Edward the Confessor on
the grille surrounding
Henry VII's tomb.

'Sirs, I here present Henry true, and rightfull, and undoubted, inheritour by the lawes of God and man to the coroune and roiall dignite of England . . . will ye, sirs, at this tyme give your willes and assentes to the same consecracion, enunccion, and coronacion?'

'Ye. Ye. Ye. So be hit. King Henry! King Henry!'

On October 30th 1485, King Henry VII, the first Tudor monarch, was magnificently crowned in Westminster Abbey. His twenty-four-year reign was to see the Abbey raised to its peak of splendour through the patronage of Henry himself and his mother, Lady Margaret Beaufort. Yet in only 30 years more it was to be ravaged, despoiled of much of its wealth and treasure, with 600 years of Roman Catholic ritual and Benedictine monasticism tossed out on history's scrap heap. In no other half-century were the ironies and treacheries of time so densely packed.

The new king prudently began his reign in a spirit of reconciliation towards the deposed houses of Lancaster and York. Elizabeth of York, his queen, daughter of Edward IV, was given her own coronation in 1487. Her mother, Elizabeth Woodville, widow of Edward IV, was restored to favour as Queen Dowager, and took a lease for forty years on Cheyneygates, the Abbot's house at Westminster where she had always taken refuge and in which the unhappy dramas of her family life had been enacted. Elizabeth had endowed a new chapel of St Erasmus, adjacent to the 13th-century Lady Chapel, where masses were to be said for the soul of Edward IV. But simultaneously both the Lady Chapel and the St Erasmus chapel were displaced in the king's imagination by the conception of a new Lady Chapel to serve as the shrine of his uncle, King Henry VI, deposed in 1461 and murdered in the Tower ten years later. His body had been buried hugger-mugger at Chertsey Abbey, by Yorkist command, probably Richard of Gloucester's. But as at the tomb of the Confessor, rumours of miracles began to circulate; he was popularly canonised as his father, Henry V, had been at Westminster, and a cult took root. Richard had the body removed to Windsor, but the cult persisted. Images of him, with lights burning before them, were set up in churches across the country. Henry Tudor shrewdly resolved to exploit this fashion, and sought Henry of Lancaster's canonisation, so that a second royal saint could lie at Westminster, to be surrounded by the tombs of the new dynasty, exactly as the Confessor's had served as the magnet for the tombs of the later medieval kings. The Tudor king, noted for his parsimony, baulked at the sum demanded by the greedy Pope Julius II for Henry's canonisation, but was not deflected from his project for a new Lady Chapel. Now that the value of Henry's remains had risen, Chertsey, Windsor and Westminster all became rivals for their possession. The dispute was heard by the Court of Star Chamber in 1498. Judgement was given in favour of Westminster, on the grounds that there was proof of Henry's intention to lie there. This decision freed the king to build his chapel.

It was a fortunate alliance of king and abbot on this cusp of change which created the Abbey's last glories. John of Islip had become a monk at Westminster on St Benedict's Day, 1480, in his 16th year, and sang his first mass in 1486, a year after Henry's accession. He became Prior in 1498, and was unanimously elected Abbot in 1500, when he was 36 years old. His election was celebrated with a modest feast and 'a potell of swet wyne, oysters, saltfish, whityngis, muskyllys, almonds and sugar'. He was a trusted friend of the king,

St Thomas of Canterbury, radiant in sunlight in Henry VII's Chapel.

1485 Richard III dies in battle at Bosworth

October 30th 1485
Coronation of Henry VII inaugurates the Tudor dynasty

January 24th 1503
Foundation of Henry VII's Lady Chapel

June 24th 1509
Coronation of Henry VIII

June 29th/July 9th 1509
Death and burial of Lady Margaret Beaufort

1532 Death and burial of Abbot Islip

1534 Thomas More in the Gatehouse Prison

1536 Seizure of the Abbey land and treasure for the king by Thomas Cromwell.

1537–40
Dissolution of the Monasteries: the Reformation in England.

1540 Surrender of the Abbey to the king.

Detail from the *Islip Roll:* Benedictine monks at prayer

Facing page: The Lady Chapel of Henry VII, built 1503–15, restored 1993–5.

Recently restored carved animals at play on the buttresses of Henry VII's Lady Chapel: *above* dog stung by a bee, *below* rabbit caught by a greyhound.

and entertained him with the marrowbone pudding for which the Abbey kitchen was celebrated, and to which Henry was particularly partial. In return Henry presented Islip with an annual gift of two tuns of wine. It was in royal company that Islip became a close friend of Thomas Wolsey, later Cardinal, who was then the king's chaplain.

Westminster's destiny could not have seemed more propitious than on January 24th 1503, when, according to John Stow's *Annals*, 'The Chappell of our ladie, above the east end of the high altar of Westminster church with also a taverne neere adioyning called the white rose, were taken downe; in the which place or plot of ground the first stone of our Lady Chappell was laid by the hands of John Islip abbot of the same monastery.' The architect-masons were almost certainly the brothers Robert and William Vertue. Robert had been in charge of building work for the king at Greenwich Palace in 1499, and with his brother had worked on Bath Abbey from 1501 to 1503. In 1501 Bishop Oliver King writes to the courtier Sir Reginald Bray, who was present at the laying of the foundation stone, that 'Robert and William Vertu have been here with me . . . they say nowe ther shall be noone so goodely neither in england nor in france. And therof

Figures of nearly a hundred saints line three sides of Henry VII's Chapel. Here is St Wilgefort, who prayed for deliverance from an arranged marriage and was given a beard.

Facing page: Henry VII's Chapel: the restored interior.

they make theym fast and sure.' Fast and sure they were. Stone from Kent, Reigate, Yorkshire and Caen was rapidly assembled and carved, and the great chapell, 'miraculum orbis' as Leland saw it, fan-vaulted to increase the span of the arches, with delicate rippling curtain walls, seeming to contain more glass than stone, was ready for consecration in 1509. Between them the king and his mother had poured the vast sum of £20,000 (£7m.) into its building and embellishment. It was to be a chantry for the House of Tudor. One hundred and seven figures of saints lined the walls, standing in judgement on the Christian soul who has just ascended the Scala Caeli, the stairway to heaven. Henry's favourite English and Welsh saints occupy dominant central positions.

But in a sequence strangely reminiscent of the Abbey's first royal builder, Edward the Confessor, its last royal builder died as soon as his work was completed. The extended solemn rituals of his funeral in the space he had lavishly created were narrated by the chronicler Edward Hall. First the body was set under a curious hearse with lights, the effigy lying upon a cushion on a large pall of gold. Next day 'were three masses solenmlie sung by bishops, and at the last masse was offered the kings baner and courser, his coat of arms, his sword, his target, and his helme, and at the end of masse the mourners offered up rich palles of cloath of gold . . . and when the quire sang "Libera me", the bodie was put into the earth.' At the graveside, the royal stewards broke their staves of office before the vault was sealed, and 'all the herauds did cast their cote armours and did hange them upon the rayles of the herse: crying lamentably in ffrench "Le Noble roi Henri le Septieme est mort", and assoone as they had so done, everie heraud put on his cote-armor againe and cryed with a loud voyce: "Vive le noble Henri le Huitesme, Roy d'Angleterre ed de France, Sire d'Ireland".'

Henry's will ordered 10,000 masses to be said 'for the remision of our synnes, and the weale of our soule', and the college of clergy and laity to pray for the repose of his soul 'as long as the world shall endure'. But a king's power to command the future ceases with his breath: his will restates the intention 'right shortly to translate the bodie and reliques of our uncle of blessed memorie', and also specified that his own tomb should stand before the high altar. But the central space is empty; Henry VIII may have reserved it for himself, or even for 'St Henry of Lancaster'. But Henry VI was never canonised, and the impulse for his translation from Windsor died with the king. There is a hollowness at the heart of Henry's Chapel, witness to the dialectic of historical change; all he could bequeath was tangible: 'the greatest image of our Lady that we now have in our Jewelhouse', and other ornaments 'to be of such as appertain to the gift of a Prince'. He required the stained glass to be emulated at Henry VI's foundation in Cambridge, in the Chapel of King's College. The glass at Cambridge remains, Westminster's has gone, victim to the ideology of the Long Parliament in 1641. The elegiac mood prompted by the death of one royal patron was deepened by the death of another on St Peter's Day in 1509. After the coronation of

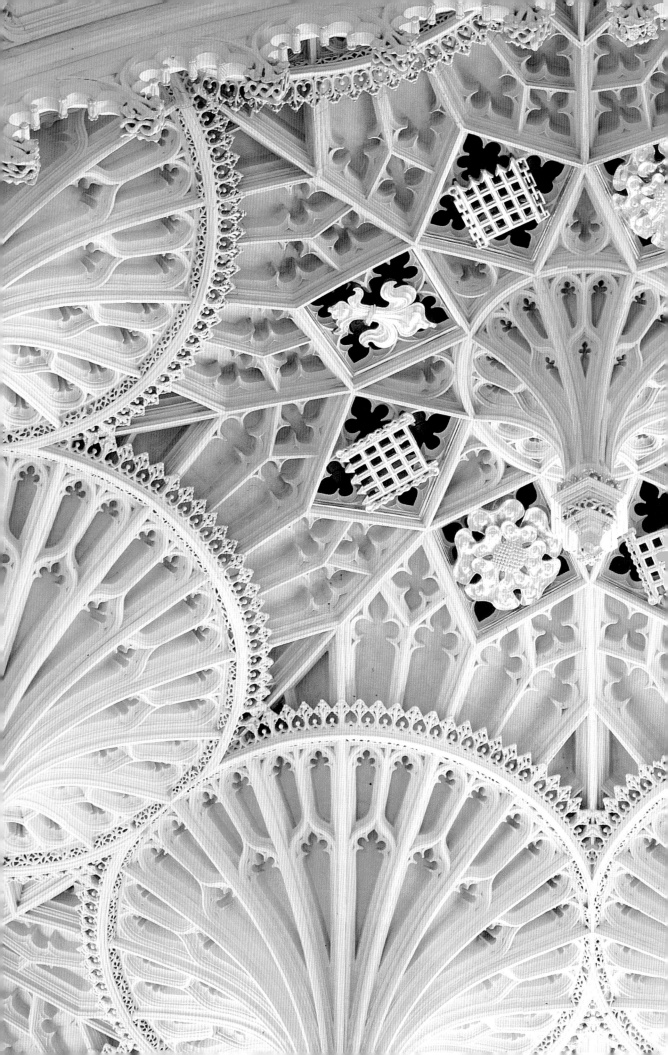

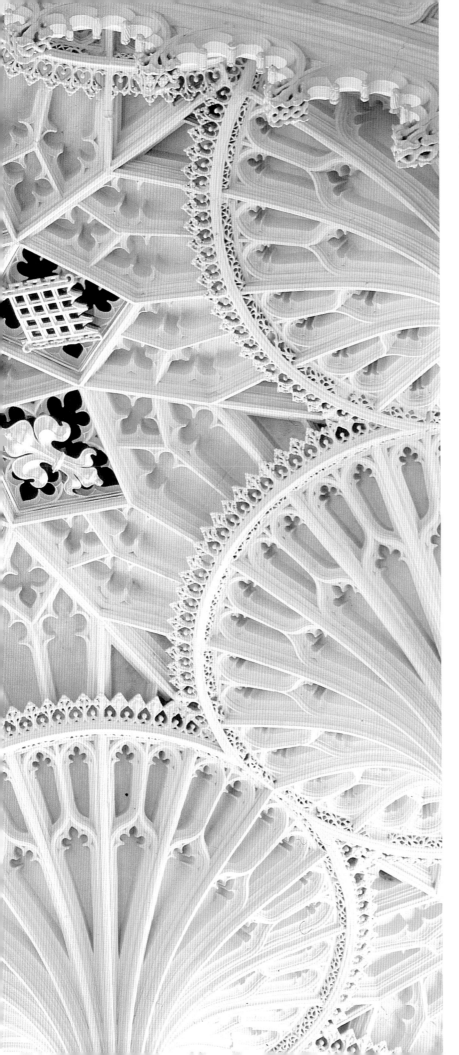

'Miraculum orbis' — a wonder of the world — was how the contemporary historian John Leland greeted Henry VII's Lady Chapel.

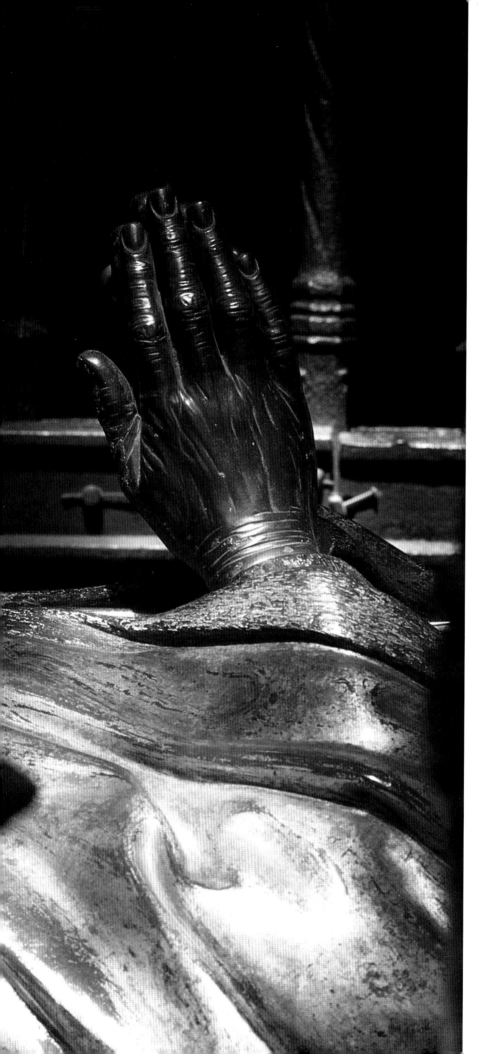

Above and left:
Torrigiano, who worked — and fought — with Michelangelo, was commissioned to create the tombs of Henry VII and his mother, Lady Margaret Beaufort. Her tomb in the South Aisle of the chapel her son constructed is unsurpassed among the Abbey's monuments.

Henry VIII and Catherine of Aragon, Lady Margaret Beaufort, mother and grandmother to the first two Tudor kings, moved to Cheyneygates, the Abbot's house in Westminster. There, during a round of coronation festivity, she died, poisoned by a cygnet she had eaten. Her body lay in the refectory until her funeral on July 9th. Erasmus wrote her epitaph; Fisher spoke her eulogy. 'Every one that knew her loved her, and everything that she said or did became her.' Torrigiano was soon to create for her the noblest and most human of the Abbey's monuments in the south aisle of her son's chapel.

It was the end of the alliance of Palace and Monastery. The new king showed Westminster no favour, and Abbot Islip prudently withdrew from all but nominal aspects of public life, devoting himself instead to the finishing of the nave: the glazing of the windows, completed in 1510 with the west window (at a cost of £44); the paving of the floor (1510–17), and the carving of the screens (1524–8). He continued, however, to be closely associated with Wolsey, sharing with him the desire both to suppress heresy and to reform monastic life. He assisted Wolsey to stage his own 'coronation' when he was made a cardinal in 1515. On November 15th his cardinal's hat was conducted in procession from Blackheath through London to Westminster with great triumph. The hat rested on the high altar until the Sunday following, when the confirmation of his high dignity was 'executed by all the bisshopes and abbottes nyghe or abought london in riche myters and coopes and other costly ornaments wche was done in so solempne a wyse as I have not seen the lyke unless it had been at the coronacion of a myghti prynce or kyng.' During the benediction Wolsey 'lay grovelling' before the altar, and then the hat was placed on his head. John Colet, Dean of St Paul's, preached on the subject of humility. Cardinals, like Christ, came not to be ministered unto, but to minister; 'whoever shall exalt himself shall be abased'.

Wolsey fell. At his downfall Islip too was in danger because of their friendship, despite having been a compliant ecclesiastical lawyer in declaring the papal dispensation permitting Henry to marry Catherine of Aragon, his brother's widow, null and void. Islip was subject to a series of accusations under the Statute of Praemunire, but escaped punishment because of the king's unexpected sentimentality towards 'the good old father'. But his position was undermined; from 1531 an annual bribe was being paid by the Abbey to Thomas Cromwell, and Henry's sentimentality did not inhibit him from taking a swathe of Abbey land and property on which to extend his Palace of Whitehall, newly acquired from the disgraced Wolsey.

The flayed St Bartholomew, on the grille of Henry VII's tomb, holds his own skin draped over his arm.

The Tudor rose of Henry VIII is flanked by the pomegranate emblem of Catherine of Aragon, his first wife, at the entrance to the chapel completed early in his reign.

Matthew Paris sketched the Westminster bells — 'Old Marie, Jesus, Edward, Holy Trinity, Le Agas'. But some were later seized by Henry VIII to turn into cannon for the French Wars.

Thomas Wolsey, friend of Abbot Islip, staged a triumphant 'coronation' for himself in the Abbey in 1515, when he was created a cardinal. After his disgrace and death, his Palace of Whitehall was taken by Henry VIII for himself.

The king had developed a taste for Abbey property earlier in his reign. From Henry III's reign, there was a bell tower, separate from the main church, at the heart of the Westminster sanctuary. Here hung bells with individual names: Old Marie, Jesus, Edward, Holy Trinity, Le Agas. Simon Simeonis, a travelling monk, visited in 1322 and reported 'Here are two bells the first in the world for size and of admirable sound.' Edward III rebuilt it, and placed in it bells to be rung on coronation days and royal funerals. 'Their ringing sowered all the drinke in the town,' growsed one citizen who preferred real ale to royalty. By the bell tower was a fountain which at coronations and great triumphs was made to run with wine out of diverse spouts. But by 1600 that corner of merrie England had run dry. Norden, the historian, looked back on 'a tower, wherein was a bell of wonderful bigness, weighing, as is reported, 33000 cwt (*sic*) and was rung only at coronations, which bell King Henry VIII employed to other uses' [euphemism for cannon fodder] 'at his going to Boulogne'.

John Islip, his world ebbing from him, died at his manor of Neyte in May 1532, and was buried in the Jesus Chapel, a chantry chapel north of the Sacrarium, which he had been building for him-

'Eye Slip' frieze: John Islip, last great abbot of the monastery, was buried in 1532 in a Chantry Chapel he had prepared for himself in the North Ambulatory. The frieze contains visual puns upon his name. Here an eye precedes a slip—a shoot pulled from a tree.

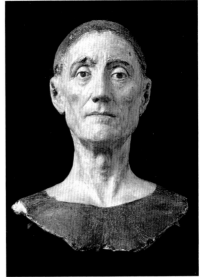

The head of Henry VII's funeral effigy, so lifelike that it must have been modelled from a death mask.

self for two years. On the day of his funeral his body was carried from Neyte to the Abbey, escorted by his monks, and so great a crowd of citizens that the whole roadway from Chelsea to Westminster was filled. It was as if all recognised that an order of life had ended. The funeral proceedings combined gravity and epicureanism. 'Then Dirige began, solemnly sung by the said monastery, and divers Diriges done in other places of the church: which being done with the other ceremonies, the mourners departed unto a place over the Chappell of the defuncte, where was prepared for them spiced breads, suchett, marmylate, spiced plate, and dyversse sorts of wines plentie. And in

The first of the Tudors in death: the Torrigiano monument of Henry VII and Elizabeth of York, in Henry VII's Lady Chapel.

Abbot Islip's Funeral Roll of
1532 is the source of the earliest
representational images of the
Abbey. This is his hearse in
place before the High Altar.

Sir Thomas More, imprisoned in
the abbot's house in 1534.

the meane ceason they of the church did burye the defuncte in the
seid Chappell of his buyldynge . . . which being done every man
departed for that night.' The event has left us the first eye-witness
images of the Abbey interior in the Funeral Roll of Abbot Islip.

Within hours of his death the first act of the English
Reformation, the Submission of the Clergy, had become law; on the
day of his funeral Sir Thomas More surrendered the Great Seal as
Lord Chancellor to Henry VIII. The Act of Submission and Act of
Supremacy were passed in the Chapter House at Westminster; on a
table there was to be the Black Book, determining the end of all the
monasteries of England. The last meeting there of the secular
Commons that had passed the statutes determining the revolution of
the Church in England was held on the day of Henry VIII's own death
in 1547.

After Islip's death the pace of events quickens, as of a current
sensing a waterfall. For a year the abbacy was left vacant, during
which time John Fulwell, monk-bailiff and treasurer, is seen report-
ing direct to Thomas Cromwell in the manner of an ingratiating spy:
'all things within the monastery are in due order, according to the
advertisement you gave me when I was last with you in London. At
your return I trust you shall not hear but that we shall deserve the
King's most gracious favour in our suit.' He is presumably anxious
to succeed Islip. But the place went to William Boston, from
Peterborough, the first abbot chosen from without in over 300 years.
It is unlikely that he was elected by the monks. We shortly catch him
out assigning offices to raise money for which he is bound to Thomas
Cromwell and William Powlet, controller of the Royal Household.

In April 1534, Sir Thomas More was committed to Boston's
custody in the Gatehouse Prison for refusing to
swear to the King's supremacy. More's letter to his
daughter, Margaret Roper, reveals the triumph in the
abbot of pragmatic self-interest over principle.
When More told him it was against his conscience
to acknowledge the supremacy, 'Then saide my
Lord of Wesminster to me, yt how sower ye matter
semed unto mine owne minde, I had cause to fere
that mine owne minde was erroniouse, when I se
the gret counsail of the realme determine of my
minde the contrary, and that therefore I ought to
change my consciens.' Boston deserves to be
revered as the patron saint of trimmers. He
complied in 1536 with Cromwell's order which
undermined the structure of monastic life: the concentration of offices and responsibilities in the
hands of the Abbot alone, the forbidding of any
monk to be absent from the community without the
Abbot's leave — an order insidiously modified by a
clause stating that if the Abbot see fit, a monk may
be allowed leave to reside outside the monastery so
long as he keeps himself from doubtful society. So

the bonds of the community were loosened by auto-
cracy, liberty — and temptation. Noble ladies and
honest dames might be received in the house of the
Abbot even in his absence.

In July 1536 Cromwell ordered the removal of
shrines, relics and images. The gold feretory surrounding the Confessor's coffin vanished into the Royal
Treasury. The king helped himself to the Abbey's traditional manors, Neyte, Ebury and Hyde, as well as to
Covent Garden. The monastery's heart had ceased to
beat. The last item in the Sacrist's roll, for the Lady Day
quarter of 1536 reads: 'Item for paynted pieces sett in to the west
wyndowe and some of coloryd glass in other wyndowes . . . xii d.'
The completion of the fabric coincided with the death of the community. Smaller houses around the country were first dissolved, then
came the turn of the greater. On January 16th 1540 there was an
assembly in the Chapter House. Boston and twenty six monks signed
the document in which 'unanimously and of their own free will',
they surrendered their church and monastery to 'thet most excellent
prince, the Lord King Henry'.

'A glittering semi-magical world
of beauty and credulity': relics
depicted in the Litlyngton Missal.

Its yearly value was £3,977 6s. 4d., second only to Glastonbury
in riches. The inventory of relics and other dissolution inventories
evoke a glittering semi-magical world of beauty and credulity, of
craftsmanship and charlatanism, of items gathered together to make a
final bow before dispersal, like the contents of an eccentric stately
home passing in turn under the auctioneer's vulgar hammer.
'Banners, streamers, quysshyns, frynges, pendents, albs, copes, chez-
abelles, septers, frontelles, plate, mitres, basonnes, altar hangings of
cloth of gold worked with lions and fleur de lys, 16 copes of cloth of
gold ('taken for the king's use'), a Redd sumpter cloth moche eaten
with rattis, one sylver spone wyth God and the worlede in hys hande,
an olde playne Towell, a greate bell candelstyke with a nose to put
on, a grete large blankette mothe eton, ii old horses wherof one ys
blind, a dong forke, ii greate tubbes to water fyshe in, a cuppe of
golde withe stonys with the blood of owre Lorde, a grete parte of the
holy crosse, a lytle coffre of sylver and gylte and berell with the heer
of Mary Mawdalen, a lytle relyke lyke a lanterne with a relyke of the
vestment of saynt petre, a rounde ball of crystall therwith to polysh
and clense the Saphyr in saynt Edwardys Rynge, a mandrake's root in
fasshion of a crosse with the ymage of owre lord annixyd to the same
crusified, the legge of saynt george with the foote cloosyde in sylver.'
These and thousands of items more were suddenly gone, together
with the way of life which bestowed on their comic arbitrariness a
collective meaning. At the dissolution assembly old Thomas Elfryd, a
monk for nearly fifty years, requested simply to be buried by the south
door, in what was 'sometyme the procession waye'. Here, in his long
sleep, he would have time to dream that he heard the feet of the
monks passing and repassing to and from the offices, from matins to
compline, sung by the black-robed Benedictines for nearly 600 years
in this place, now silenced, it seemed, forever.

A photograph taken in the
chapel of St Nicholas seems to
record a ghostly monk at vigil.

'That antique pile behold
Where royal heads receive the sacred gold;
It gives them crowns, and does their ashes keep;
There, made like gods—like mortals, there they sleep.
Making the circle of their reign complete,
These suns of empire, where they rise, they set.'

Edmund Waller

Protestant martyr 1555.

All Turned Upside Down

1540–1660: Revolution in Church and State

Westminster Abbey and the river-side Royal Palace from the east in the time of Henry VIII. A conjectural reconstruction by H. W. Brewer (19th century).

The Abbey was empty. There is no record of any activity there from January to December 1540. Twenty years later, from July 1559 until May 1560, it was empty again. Two such stillnesses, the blanknesses of shock following the overturning of everything familiar, mark the beginning and end of a period of turbulence in the relations of Church and State so violent that the survivors seem grateful merely to have been so. One hundred years on, and the equivalent double decade, from 1640 to 1660, releases a second wave of mere anarchy, spread wider still through the convulsion of civil war, during which the continuance of Church or State in any form often seemed unimaginable. And even between those times of turmoil, the tensions of religious and secular, Court and Parliament, Anglican and Puritan, one powerful aspiring man against another, make for a sustainedly fractious phase of national and local life. It seems especially important to recall that what we from our safe distance see as shapely was to the participants inchoate and perilous.

In December 1540 letters patent were issued to convert the Abbey into a Cathedral, and a royal warrant instructed Cranmer to consecrate Thomas Thirlby, Bishop of Westminster. In August 1542 the patent of endowment and the statutes of the new collegiate church were confirmed. As its title tells us, the new order at Westminster took as its model a community of scholars rather than the Benedictine family devoted to monastic offices and the ideal of brotherhood. It was headed by the Dean, supported by a chapter of twelve prebendaries, and its structure included twelve 'petty canons', a grammar school with a master, usher and forty scholars, a choral foundation of twelve singing men and ten choristers, twelve almsmen, and an obligation to provide stipends for ten professors and twenty students at Oxford and Cambridge. The Dean and Chapter were allotted an endowment from the former monastic lands which produced an income of about £2,500 a year. Abbot Boston, an instinctive survivor, reverted to his family name of Benson and became Dean. Six monks who had served under him in the last years of the monastery reappeared as prebendaries. From 1542 until 1556 the Abbey was directed by this new Chapter.

The death of Henry VIII in January 1547 and the succession of his 10-year-old son as Edward VI opened wider the gates to anarchy. At his coronation in the Abbey on February 20th, the Archbishop of Canterbury and Protector Somerset jointly placed the crown on the boy's head. The precocious child, presented with the three swords representing the three kingdoms, declared that there was one lacking, and called for a Bible. 'That', he said, 'is the sword of the Spirit . . . without that sword we are nothing; we can do nothing . . . from that alone we obtain all power, virtue, grace, salvation, and whatsoever we have of Divine strength.' Edward lay prostrate on the altar while his back was anointed. The sense of his frailty prompted Cranmer's

February 20th 1547
Coronation of Edward VI

October 1st 1553 Coronation of Mary I (Mary Tudor)

1556 Monastery re-established: John Feckenham, *Abbot*

1557
Confessor's shrine restored

January 15th 1559
Coronation of Elizabeth I

1559
Final dissolution of monastery

May 21st 1560 Foundation of Collegiate Church by Elizabeth I

July 25th 1603
Coronation of James I

1604–11 Authorised version of the Bible prepared in the Jerusalem Chamber

1618 Imprisonment and execution of Sir Walter Raleigh

1620 John Williams, *Dean*

1621 William Laud, *Prebendary*

February 2nd 1626
Coronation of Charles I

1642 Start of English Civil War leading to the execution of the king and establishment of the Commonwealth

1642–3 Seizure of Regalia, destruction of stained glass

January 29th 1649
Execution of Charles I

1649-60
The Commonwealth: Oliver Cromwell, Lord Protector

1658 Death of Cromwell

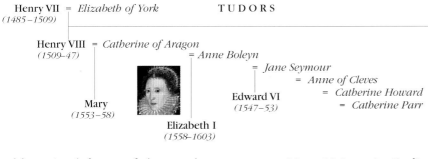

Henry VII = *Elizabeth of York*   **T U D O R S**
(1485–1509)

Henry VIII = *Catherine of Aragon*   *Margaret = James IV of Scotland*
(1509–47)   = *Anne Boleyn*
                              = *Jane Seymour*
                                   = *Anne of Cleves*   *James V*
                    Edward VI   = *Catherine Howard*   *of Scotland*
Mary   *(1547–53)*   = *Catherine Parr*
(1553–58)
          Elizabeth I   *Mary Queen of Scots = Henry Stuart*
          (1558–1603)

                                                                    S T U A R T S

address in defence of the royal supremacy. 'Your Majesty is God's Viceregent, and idolatry, the tyranny of the Bishops of Rome, is to be banished from your subjects, and images removed.' A brave but hollow declaration of a common purpose. In 1550 ecclesiastic politics, chiefly the hostility of Ridley, Bishop of London, and Cox, the new Dean, secured the suppression of the bishopric of Westminster and the removal of Thirlby, though he, another consummate survivor lucky enough to be abroad on diplomatic business whenever there was a political crisis at home, succeeded in serving Henry, Edward and Mary before being deprived of his position by Elizabeth because of his refusal to conform to the Anglican services her policy required.

James I (*VI of Scotland*)
(1603–25)

Charles I
(1625–49)

Commonwealth
(1649–60)

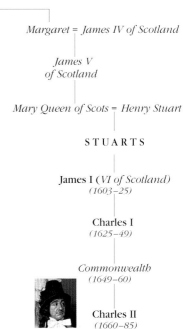

Charles II
(1660–85)

John Norden's Map of
Westminster, 1593.

Philip I of Spain and Mary Tudor,
enclosed within the giant
illuminated letter 'P' in
the Abbey Charter of 1556.

In 1553 the sickly young king died, and the edgy, precarious Anglican interlude with him. The public heaviness of heart at the threat embodied in his Catholic half-sister, Mary I, is caught by Henry Machyn, citizen and vivid diarist of London in the 1550s. 'At hys bereing was the grettest mone mad for hym of ys deth as ever was hard or sene, boyth of all sorts of pepull, wepyng and lamentyng.' Cranmer conducted the funeral service in the Abbey from the new prayer book of the reformed English Church, though he must have known that his day was done. Afterwards in the Tower, with Mary present, a Requiem Mass was celebrated by the Bishop of Winchester 'after the old Popish form'.

For her coronation in October 1553, Mary was obsessed with purging the heresy of the Protestant interregnum. She required a fresh supply of holy oil and a new coronation chair blessed by Pope Julius III, lest either had been defiled by Edward's use. The Abbey as a whole was scrubbed out as if polluted. 'For good wyffe Wyllet and mother Syllybarne for making cleane Kyng H the VII's tombe wt sope and watr II days . . . iis.' Dean Cox had been purged too; in August he had been arrested on suspicion of plotting, sent to the Marshalsea Prison, and deprived of his offices. He managed to flee to Frankfurt. Nine other Abbey prebendaries were also deprived, and took thankful refuge abroad. Four days after her coronation, after opening her first parliament, Mary rode to the Abbey to hear Mass, dressed in scarlet velvet. Two bishops present refused to kneel during the elevation of the Host, and were manhandled out of the church. But the monastery was not immediately restored, probably because of the constraint of royal finances. The Dean and Chapter, now officiating at Catholic rituals, survived ingloriously until 1556. A Chapter minute for January 17th of that year exposes the comic contentiousness that the times fostered. 'Wheras Sir Edwarde Hamonde, pryste, did breake John Wodes heade, beinge one of the clarkes, with a pote, he was commandyd to the gate howse for the space of iij? dayes by Mr Deanes comandement and payde to John Wode for the healinge of his heade xl s. by the decree of Mr Deane and the chapiter.'

Mr Dean's commandment had little longer to run. In September 1556 he and his chapter were abolished and John Feckenham, Dean of St Paul's, proposed himself as abbot of the restored monastery. The charter re-establishing Benedictine possession was dated November 10th 1556. Machyn watched the proceedings on November 21st: 'The sam day was the new abbot of Westmynster putt in, docthur Fecknam, late dene of Powlles and xiiii moo monks shorne in: and the morrow after the lord abott with ys coventt whentt a prossessyon after the old fassyon in ther monkes 'wede, in cowles of blake say.'

In December he saw a sanctuary procession staged to affirm the old custom. 'And thus was the Abbey restored to its Pristin Privileges.' Restoring the shrine of the Confessor to its pristine condition, however, was impossible. The gold had been seized for the Royal Treasury in 1536; after the Dissolution the structure had been partly dismantled and the saint's body concealed. But Feckenham patched together what he could, provided a new wooden gabled structure to house the coffin, and on March 20th 1557 the Confessor's third translation was celebrated. Machyn was there, breathlessly: 'The xx day of Marche was taken up agayn with a hondered lyghtes kyng Edward the confessor in the sam plasse wher ys shryne was and ytt shalle be sett up agayne as fast as my lord abbott can have ytt done for yt was a godly shyte [sight] to have see yt how reverently he was cared from the plasse that he was taken up wher he was led [laid] when that the abbay was spowlyd and robyd and so he was caried and goodly syngyng and senssyng as has bene sene, and masse song.'

But despite the power of Feckenham's sermons in the Abbey and in the open air at St Paul's Cross, as he sought to win back the citizens' devotion to the old faith, there was no popular support for the Catholic Church or for monasticism. The number of monks at Westminster had risen to forty by 1558, but tales told against them were readily believed. In August 1557 Anne of Cleves, fourth wife of Henry VIII, was buried with full Catholic ritual, but when the hearse was taken down, it was found that 'the monks by night had spoiled [it] of all velvett cloth, armes, baners, penselles, and all the majesty and valens, the wyche was never sene afore so done.'

Mary Tudor died, childless, on November 17th 1558. Her death lifted a great weight from the city. 'All the churches in London did ring, and at night men did make bonfires and set tables in the street, and did eat, and drink, and make merry for the new queen.' At the Abbey too for over 300 years November 17th, Elizabeth I's accession day, was celebrated as Foundation Day, when the bells rang in

The tomb of Henry III, seen from the North Ambulatory, with the Confessor's shrine behind it. The gold mosaic pieces within reach have been picked away by visitors down the ages.

A drawing by Anthony van den Wyngaerde, c. 1555, of a Westminster still largely a royal island surrounded by open space.

St Margaret's Churchyard was a convenient public space for the disposal of traitors and heretics. William Flower, martyred in 1555, preceded by 110 years the burial of the remains of some of the regicides of 1649 in a common pit near this spot.

gratitude and relief at liberation from uncertainty and for a lasting rebirth into its Anglican destiny. John Strype, the historian, captures that mood exactly in his praise of the new queen: 'she rusheth not in at the first chop, to violate and breach former laws; to stir her people to change what they list, before Order be taken by Law. She hangeth no Man, she beheadeth none, she burneth none, spoileth none.' It is like waking from a nightmare to find a benign morning. Mary's hearse was taken to the Abbey on December 13th, and her funeral Mass and burial took place next day. 'Ladies riding all in black trailed to the ground, and a hundred poor men in good black gowns bore long torches with hoods on their heads, and arms on them. And all the way chandlers having torches to supply them that had their torches burnt out.' She had been crowned by the Bishop of Winchester—though his right to do so was never established—and now, as a man at bay, he preached a funeral sermon which caused such displeasure that he was put under house arrest. 'She restored to the Church such ornaments as in the time of Schism were taken away and spoiled. She found the Realm poisoned with Heresy, and purged it.' She was buried in the North aisle of Henry VII's Lady Chapel, where her officers broke their staves and cast them down into the grave. But outside the church there was no solemnity. 'The People plucked down the Cloth, every man a Piece that could catch it, round about the Church, and the Arms too.' Souvenir hunting is no new phenomenon. And even the principals were disposed to festivity. 'The Queen being buried the Archbishop of York came and declared a Collation, and as soon as he had made an end, all the trumpets blew a blast. And then the Chief Mourners, the Lords and Knights, the Bishops and the Abbot went into the Abby to Dinner.' Only Abbot Feckenham was in no mood to enjoy his collation: his funeral address was a stoical elegy for his religion and himself: 'And now it only remaineth that we look and provide for ourselves and, seeing these daily casualties of death, gather our faculties and put ourselves in a readiness to die.'

But first he had to put on a brave face for Elizabeth's coronation on January 15th 1559. The popular mood was ecstatic. 'Such was the shout and the noise of organs, fifes, trumpets, drums and bells, that it seemed as though the world had come to an end.' But the service had its difficulties. Because of the death of Cardinal Pole on the same day as the queen, there was no Archbishop of Canterbury. Nicholas Heath, Archbishop of York, refused to perform the office because of

Elizabeth's aversion to Rome. Owen Oglethorpe, Bishop of Carlisle, was persuaded to crown the queen, but affronted all his brother bishops by doing so, and later was said to have died of remorse. 'It was a display to cheer a cold January, all the trumpets, and knights, and lords, and heralds of arms in their coat armours, and all the bishops, mitred in scarlet, and all the street laid with gravel, and blue cloth unto the abbey, and railed on every side, and all the chapel singing "Salve Festa Dies", so to the abbey to mass and there her grace was crowned.' Elizabeth complained that the oil 'was grease and smelt ill' (perhaps it was her half-sister's Catholic oil), and when the Host was elevated during Mass, she was offended, and withdrew to her private room. But, however chancily, the ritual was completed, and then everyone went to Westminster Hall to dinner. The queen knew how precarious her life had been, and how fortunate she was to attain this day. Her prayer on going to her coronation is that of a dazed survivor: 'O Lord almightie and everlasting God, I give thee most hartie thanks, that thou has been mercifull unto me, as to spare me to behold this joyful day. And I acknowledge that thou has dealt as wonderfully and as mercifully with me, as thou didst with thy true and faithful servant Daniel thy prophet, whom thou deliveredst out of the den from the cruelty of the greedy and raging lions, even so was I overwhelmed, and only by thee delivered.'

Elizabeth I's coronation procession in January 1559.

College Hall, the Abbot's State
Dining-room, completed by
Nicholas Litlyngton in 1375, now
used by Westminster School. The
High Table is backed by the arms
of Westminster, Christ Church,
Oxford and Trinity College,
Cambridge.

Facing page: Queen Elizabeth I,
a contemporary portrait that
hangs in Westminster School.

Irreverent visitors, including
Westminster schoolboys,
have sought immortality by
carving their names on the
Coronation Chair.

'All things are turned upside down', complained Feckenham
to Parliament in January 1559. In May all religious houses were again
dissolved, and the monks of Westminster finally put away their black
robes. On May 21st 1560, the Queen's Commissioners were authorised to give possession of Westminster Abbey to Dean Bill and a
chapter of twelve prebendaries, and conferred upon the Abbey a new
charter which in essence reaffirmed the provisions first made by her
father, Henry VIII, in 1542. Bill was installed as Dean on June 30th,
and at last a settled order was launched. Elizabeth was attached both
to the Abbey, where she habitually attended services after openings
of Parliament, and to the grammar school established in the 1542
charter. Its scholars, poor but talented children of Westminster, were,
under the Charter, part of the collegiate foundation. More than once
she and her Council came to College Hall, the state dining-room of
the 14th-century Abbot's House, to see the scholars perform plays in
Latin by Plautus and Terence. For a visit in 1587 the boys compiled
in her honour a volume of Latin poems and epigrams which was
presented to her. Here the civil servants, diplomats, divines and
scholars fit for her aspiring state were to be educated: Richard Hakluyt
the geographer, Ben Jonson the dramatist, Robert Cotton the
antiquarian, George Herbert the poet. Over the years, the school
prospered, and grew. A dozen or so boys in the Almonry School
became forty scholars under Henry VIII; the school's reputation for
learning, and its function as a ladder of preferment to Christ Church,
Oxford and Trinity College, Cambridge, by Elizabeth's command, soon
attracted both boarders and day boys. By the 18th century it was the
most fashionable school in England, with more than four hundred
pupils. Though Dean and Chapter retained control of it until the
Public Schools Act of 1868 brought about a grateful divorce, the
Abbey must often have found it a bitter pill to swallow as they suffered the unforeseen consequences of monastic charity. A community of turbulent boys in the very heart of the precinct was the antithe-
sis of all order and decorum, and there were scores of occasions when
the Chapter must have wished their inconvenient cuckoo painlessly
dislodged. Robert Uvedale in 1658 darted through the crowd at
Cromwell's funeral to snatch the silk pall covering the bier; in the 18th
century the boys treated the Abbey as their playground: 'many idle
boys' are disorderly in the Cloisters, and a beadle has to be appointed; they climb over the wall into the orchard, so the wall has to be
raised; they break all the windows, so Dr Knipe, headmaster, is
ordered to admonish them; they go up to the belfry and cut the lock
on the door to the tower; a large fence is erected to keep them from
Dr Blair's brewhouse. In 1740 N. Curzon, R. Assheton, N. Lister and
T. Pelham carve their names on the Coronation Chair to celebrate their
sleeping in it overnight, presumably on different occasions. In 1766
Andrews reaches into a dilapidated tomb and steals the jawbone of
Richard II. In the 19th century they conduct fist fights in the Cloister
Garth and disturb the services; they play violent games of hockey
round the Cloisters and damage the monuments. Burton and
Markham climb over the roofs in the belief, so they say, that Dean

The tomb of Lord Hunsdon, cousin to Elizabeth I, is the most extravagant of the many Tudor and Jacobean tombs to displace the altars in the chapels formerly used by Benedictine monks for celebrating Mass.

Buckland's pet monkey was loose, and demolish Mr Turle the organist's chimney; the Abbey parapet is the very place for smoking cigars and watching fires. Security is tightened and in the 1990s furtive cigarettes have to be puffed in canonical doorways in Little Cloister, but scaffolding is ever a challenge, and a housemaster's pyjamas have been flown from the flagpole on the north-west tower. At ground level the scruffy dress and scruffier language favoured by the youth of the 1990s thrusts raffishness upon the precinct, and a mixture of energy, ignorance and self-absorption can still see canons and their families trampled down in the Cloister by a rumbustious swarm of adolescents. And yet there they still are, the scholars, clad in white surplices in formal processions, incubi who resist exorcism, for successive projects to move the school elsewhere have come to nothing. Sometimes they have even been useful: fighting fires, repelling riots, acclaiming the monarch as they have at every coronation since that of James II in 1685. They were not at their best for Queen Victoria in 1838, however, when an acerbic Chapter minute records that 'the Westminster boys were removed from the situation that before they generally occupied in the organ loft, and were placed in a gallery in the south side of it. It might have been as well had they been banished entirely from the Abbey, for a more murderous scream of recognition than that which they gave HM Queen Victoria yesterday was never before heard by civilised ears.' As financial pressures have pushed up numbers to nearly 700, the only recourse for a Dean and Chapter in a disgruntled mood would seem to be a stoical acceptance of the school as, at worst, 'the spot of dirt without which the whole will not cohere', or at best, an infallible remedy for excessive dignity. The truth is that in recent years relations between Abbey and School have been remarkably creative, artistically and socially. Six hundred years of contingency appear to have culminated in symbiosis.

Elizabeth's death at Richmond in 1603 was followed by a sumptuous procession to Westminster, and funeral there, the first

Funeral of Queen Elizabeth I, 1603, showing her funeral effigy lying on top of her coffin.

royal funeral of which a visual record survives. On April 28th 'the corpse, imbalmed, lapped in lead covered with purple velvet, laid on a chariot, drawn by four great horses, trapt in black velvet, the picture of her whole body, counterfeited after life, in her parliament robes with a crown on her head and a sceptre in her hand, lying on the corpse . . . was roylly conveyed to the Collegiate Church of St Peter of Westminster. There were esteemed mourners in black about the numbers of one thousand six hundred persons.'

Elizabeth I was the last monarch buried in the Abbey to have a monument erected above her, embellished by the goldsmith and painter Nicholas Hilliard. The destruction of the monastic altars in 1561 was an invitation to great courtiers to build swaggering tombs in their place, intrusions vulgar both in size and style, like *nouveau riche* mansions, images of arrogance, vanity, power and wealth. The tomb of the queen's cousin, Lord Hunsdon, in the Chapel of St John the Baptist, wins first prize in every category. Death was crowding into the place. 'Here's an acre sown indeed/ With the richest, royallest seed/ That the earth could e'er suck in . . .'

The replacement crown on the marble figure of Elizabeth I, caught in this picture, was in place for only an hour or two before being snatched away by a souvenir hunter.

The tomb of Mary Queen of Scots, mother of James I, in the South Aisle of Henry VII's Chapel. James had Mary's body brought from Peterborough in 1612 for burial in the Abbey. The position and scale of the tomb express deliberate rivalry with that of Elizabeth, who consented to Mary's execution at Fotheringay Castle in 1587.

The ferocious lion at the foot of Mary Queen of Scots' tomb is more than a match for the English.

The Abbey seemed to catch and hold the temper we think of as Jacobean: melancholy, violent, death preoccupied; innocence, ideals, energy spent. Francis Beaumont's trite lines darken when the great preacher Jeremy Taylor reworks them into a chilling *memento mori*: 'Where our kings are crowned, their ancestors lie interred, and they must walk over their grandsire's head to take his crown. There is an acre sown with royal seed; the copy of the greatest change from rich to naked, from ceiled roofs to arched coffin, from living like gods to die like men. There is enough to cool the flames of lust; to abate the height of pride; to appease the itch of covetous desires; to sully and dash out the dissembling colours of a lustful, artificial and imaginary beauty. There the warlike and the peaceful, the fortunate and the miserable, the beloved and the despised princes mingle their dust, and pay down their symbol of mortality; and tell all the world that, when we died, our ashes shall be equal to kings, and our accounts easier, and our pains or our crowns shall be less.'

At Westminster during James's reign there was matter enough to deepen darkness and preoccupy soothsayers. Though his coronation was the first to use English throughout rather than Latin, there were few to celebrate it, for, because of an outbreak of plague, people were forbidden to gather in London. In 1612 James brought the body of his mother, Mary Queen of Scots, executed by Elizabeth, from Peterborough Cathedral, to lie beneath a monument placed so as to rival, and designed so as to excel, that of her executioner. But less than two months later, her vault had to be opened again to receive the body of James's son, Henry, Prince of Wales, cynosure of his age, who had died of typhoid, aged only 18. A throng of two thousand mourners, deeply afflicted with grief, accompanied the body 'at a foot's pace' from palace to abbey. Henry's death promoted Prince Charles, then aged 12, as heir to the throne, and also sealed the fate of his friend, Sir Walter Raleigh, whom the king suspected of disloyalty, and who was in detention in the Tower of London. Sentenced to execution at last in 1618, he passed his last night on earth at Westminster, in the Gatehouse Prison that had from monastic days been one of the Abbot's civic responsibilities. The gaol stood above the Tothill Street gate to the precinct. An inventory of 1379 lists 'a bolt of thick iron called Saint Petrys botes with 3 iron shackles belonging thereto'. Here Thomas More had been held in 1534, and now on October 29th 1618 Raleigh was brought from the Tower to lodge there. Just before dawn his cousin, Charles Thynne, came to him and advised him about his demeanour on the scaffold. 'Take heed you goe not too much upon the brave hand, for your enemies will take exceptions at that.' Raleigh would have none of that. 'Good Charles, give me leave to be merry, for this is the last merriment that ever I shall have in this worlde: but when I come to the last parte, you will see me grave enough.' Dean Tounson went with him to the scaffold in the morning; 'he was very cheerful, eate his breakfast hertily and tooke tobacco, and made no more of his death, than if it had bene to take a journey.' As he left the Gatehouse, he was given a cup of sack. Asked if it was to his liking, he replied: "I will answer you as did the fellow who drank of St Giles's bowl as he went to Tyburn: "It is a good drink, if a man might but tarry by it.'" Raleigh left instructions that the verse he wrote during his last night in the Gatehouse should be given to Tounson:

> 'Even such is Time, that takes in trust
> Our youth, our joys, our all we have,
> And pays us but with earth and dust,
> Who in the dark and silent grave,
> When we have wandered all our ways,
> Shuts up the story of our days.
> And from that earth, that grave, that dust,
> The Lord shall raise me up, I trust.'

Sir Walter Raleigh spent the night before his execution in 1618 in the Gatehouse Prison. He is buried in St Margaret's Church.

Raleigh was buried in the chancel of St Margaret's Church, but the site is unknown. Two more literary men were to follow Raleigh to the Gatehouse during the century: the courtier-poet Richard Lovelace, committed for presenting to Parliament a petition on behalf of Charles I in 1642, and the elderly Samuel Pepys, in June 1690, on suspicion of being 'affected' to King James II. After six days, he was suffered to return to his house in regard of his indisposition. The lines Lovelace wrote, 'To Althea from Prison', in the Gatehouse, echo Raleigh's heroic insouciance and offer comfort to prisoners everywhere:

The state apartment of the Abbot, called the Jerusalem Chamber, was completed c.1380.

> 'Stone walls do not a prison make,
>   Nor iron bars a cage;
> Minds innocent and quiet take
>   That for an hermitage.
> If I have freedom in my love
>   And in my soul are free,
> Angels alone, that soar above,
>   Enjoy such liberty.'

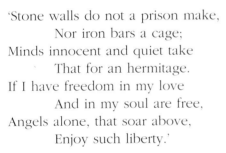

Four Westminster School boys, confined there in 1679 after the chivalrous murdering of a bailiff threatening to eject a poor woman from her lodging, left no poetic record of their restraint.

At the beginning of James's reign, different creative gifts were exercised in the Jerusalem Chamber by the beloved Dean Lancelot Andrewes and his committee of churchmen who were at work on the new translation of the Bible authorised by the Hampton Court Conference in 1604. From Genesis to the Second Book of Kings was the remit of Andrewes' group, one of six appointed to divide the scriptures between them. And in 1624 at the end of the reign, when the French Ambassadors were in

Spikiness was not confined to 17th-century politicians and clerics: this bristling porcupine is a less than ideal footrest for the Countess of Sussex in St Paul's Chapel.

Dean John Williams, a pivotal figure in the upheavals of Church and State between 1620 and 1651.

London to conclude the protracted negotiations for the marriage of Prince Charles to Henrietta Maria, English music was on show, together with the Abbey itself, in a pageant to delight all the senses: 'The Embassdors . . . were brought in at the North Gate of the Abbey, which was stuck with Flambeaux everywhere that strangers might cast their eyes upon the stateliness of the Church. At the door of the Quire the lord keeper besought their Lordships to go in and take their seats there for a while. At their entrance the organ was touched by the best finger of that age, Mr Orlando Gibbons.' After a supper in the Jerusalem Chamber, they returned to the church. 'While a verse was plaid, the Lord Keeper presented the Embassadors . . . with our Liturgy, as it spake to them in their own language. The Lord Embassadors, and their great Train, took up the Stalls, where they continued about half an hour, while the Quire Men, vested in their rich copes, with their Choristers, sung three several Anthems, with most exquisite voices, before them.'

But the pageant was insubstantial. Within weeks the king was dead in London, Orlando Gibbons dead in Canterbury while waiting for Henrietta Maria's arrival, the Lord Keeper (Dean Williams) dismissed and humiliated and King Charles I crowned in a ceremony dogged by ill-omen. James I was buried privately in Henry VII's Chapel four days before the public funeral. His setting, like his rising, was muted.

On July 10th 1620, John Williams, Dean of Salisbury, was installed as Dean of Westminster. In 1621 William Laud, an older and equally ambitious man, was appointed a prebendary. The deep, savage, obsessional animosity between them was to dominate the affairs of Church and State for over twenty years, until Laud's execution. A drama as intense as theirs cries out for an even-handed playwright; though each was championed in print by a biographer— John Hacket for Williams, Peter Heylyn for Laud—their partisanship contributes more smoke than light. Williams, a favourite of James I and Buckingham, had written to put himself forward for the Abbey: 'I trouble not your honour for Profit, but only for conveniency, for being unmarried, and inclining so to continue, I do find that Westminster is fitter by much for that disposition.' This disingenuous access to the ladder of politics was startlingly successful. Within a year of his appointment to Westminster he was made Lord Keeper of the Great Seal in succession to his friend Bacon, as well as Bishop of Lincoln. As Lord Keeper he was among the most powerful men in the land. James I had declared that he 'would have a clergyman: he would have no more lawyers, for they are all so nursed in corruption that they cannot get away from it.' Williams found the Deanery 'a lodging which afforded him marvellous quietness to turn over his papers and to serve the king'. He devoted himself unstintingly to the care of Abbey and School, spending money of his own on the fabric, transforming the standard of the music, founding the present Abbey Library, where his full-length portrait still gazes down on his carved-oak presses, establishing a discipline of sound finances (though entertaining lavishly) and taking the closest interest in the school, praising and rewarding 'the choicest wits', scattering money 'as if it had been but dung to manure their industry'. Laud's envy of so bright a star, given his own political ambition and the bitterness of having to serve under him, is inevitable. They were divided further by their churchmanship: Laud resented the austerity of services Williams preferred as dean, and took every opportunity to smear him as a closet Puritan. James's death was a bitter blow to Williams. 'The day of the Servant's Prosperity shut up and a blight of long and troublesome Adversity followed,' comments Hacket. Williams preached the king's funeral sermon, but without his patron was a prime target. 'The favour of a prince is seldom found again when it is once lost, and a cashiered courtier is an almanack of last year.' 'A perfect diocese within himself,' sneered Heylyn—'Bishop, Dean, Prebend, Residentiary, Parson—and all these at once.' As he fell, so Laud ascended. Williams was at once deprived of the Keepership, though he writes to a friend that 'you love me too well . . . to wish that I should have . . . to continue longer in this glorious miserye and splendid slaverie wherin I have lived (if a man may call such a toiling a livinge) for these five years almost.' More hurtful was his exclusion by the new king from the coronation service in his own church, and Charles's selection of Laud to act his deputy. Laud's detailed revision of the service to accommodate it 'more punctually' to the rules of the Church of England was to prove one of the signatures on his own death-warrant.

The coronation of Charles I, on Candlemas Day 1626, was, doubtless with the benefit of hindsight, pregnant with omens. There was an earthquake. The King chose to travel by water from the Tower rather than by land, for fear of plague, but his boat ran aground at Parliament stairs, and he had to scramble across other boats to reach the jetty. He indulged his own fancy for the colour of his clothes, and wore white. a colour associated with saints and martyrs, instead of the traditional purple. In the service there was a strange silence when the acclamation was invited, until the Earl of Arundel prompted the congregation to cry out 'God save King Charles'. And Senhouse, Bishop of Carlisle, taking as the text of his sermon 'And I will give unto thee a crown of life', was thought to have given 'his funeral sermon when he was alive, as if he were to have none when he was to be buried'. The Bishop's death shortly afterwards was seen to confirm his misjudgement.

Williams now needed all his Welsh and political guile to keep Laud at bay and to retain his deanery. Laud pursued him hard, appointing Heylyn, his own chaplain, as prebendary-spy in 1631, and sending in commissioners at Lincoln and Westminster to seek evidence against him. The 1635 visitation at Westminster elicited thirty- six articles of complaint, but Williams put up a fine defence, and they 'flew away over the Abbey, like a flock of wild geese, if you but cast one stone amongst them.' But in 1637 Laud, now Archbishop

The east end of the North Aisle of Henry VII's Chapel is a children's corner of tombs. In the foreground cradle is Sophia, died 1606, aged 3 days, and behind her Mary, died 1607, aged 2 years, both daughters of James I.

THO: PARR OF Y COUNTY OF SALLOP. BORNE
IN A: 1483. HE LIVED IN Y REIGNES OF TEN
PRINCES VIZ: K.EDW.4. K.ED.5. K.RICH.3.
K.HEN.7. K.HEN.8 K.EDW.6.Q.MA.Q.ELI:
K.JA.& K.CHARLES.AGED 152 YEARES.
& WAS BURYED HERE NOVEMB. 15. 1635.

'Old Parr', Thomas Parr, who claimed to be 152 years old, was brought to London from Shropshire as a celebrity, and promptly died. He was buried in the South Transept in 1635.

of Canterbury, succeeded in bringing Williams before the Court of Star Chamber on a treason charge. He was fined £10,000, suspended from office, had his property seized, and was sent to the Tower. He was lucky to survive 1638, when he was implicated in a correspondence with Lambert Osbaldston, Headmaster of Westminster School, which fell into Laud's hands. Osbaldston's obscure, half-coded words 'the little vermin the urchin and hocus-pocus is this stormy Christmas at true and real variance with the Leviathan', which Laud took to refer to himself, led to the might of Star Chamber descending on the Headmaster: 'sentenced five thousand pounds . . . and to have his ears tacked to the pillory in the presence of his scholars.'

The malice of Laud and Heylyn pursued Williams even in the Tower; for Laud there could clearly be no peace until he was dead. But the advent of the Long Parliament in 1640 brought an astonishing reversal of fortunes. In December he was released and restored to his Deanery; shortly afterwards Laud was to replace him in the Tower, and for him the only release was to be the executioner's block. Williams, returning to take his place in Abbey services, heard Peter Heylyn preach an angry sermon against the Puritans. The Dean knocked with his staff on the pulpit, crying 'No more of that point, Peter, no more of that point!' Heylyn: 'I have a little more to say, my Lord, and then I have done.'

For a few desperate months, before the kingdom dissolved into raw and dizzying anarchy, Williams found himself effectively head of the Government, attempting to mediate between King and the Puritan-inclining House of Commons, counselling Charles to sign the Earl of Strafford's death-warrant, and chairing an ecclesiastical committee to restore order in public worship. He was also appointed Archbishop of York in 1641, so, with Laud, Archbishop of Canterbury, now in the Tower in Williams's place, he was head of the English Church as well. But the task of holding together such disparate forces as were fissuring the kingdom was beyond any man.

Wenceslas Hollar's drawing of Westminster from the river, 1647.

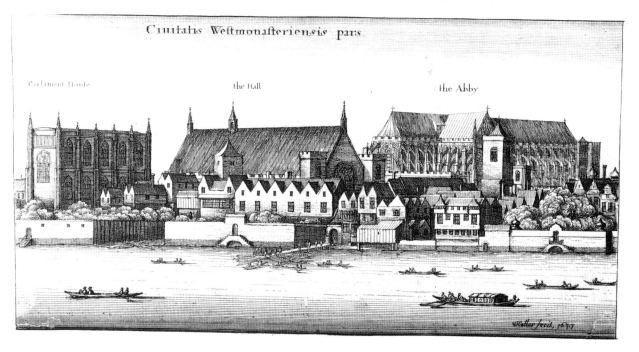

Ciuitatis Westmonasteriensis pars.

Parliament House · the Hall · the Abby

Wenceslas feat, 1647

The dissolution of the past hung about two very different burials in the 1630s. 'Old Parr', Thomas Parr, was discovered by the Earl of Arundel in Shropshire, and brought by him to London as a celebrity because he claimed to have been born in 1483, and was therefore 152 years old. At an age of over 100 he had been convicted of fornication, and for a punishment had been made to stand draped in a white sheet in Alberbury Church. He enjoyed a very brief metropolitan fame, and was shown to Charles I, but died in November 1635 of the effects of his change of scene. After his remains had been scrutinized by William Harvey, the royal physician, he was buried in the South Transept where he was later to be joined by other tellers of tales: Dickens, Hardy (who would have relished him) and Kipling.

Ben Jonson, whose childhood and schooldays had been at Westminster, came back in his old age and lived in a house between St Margaret's and Henry VII's Chapel known as the Talbot, next to the house Chaucer had once leased. Here he kept a tame fox (called Volpone?) in a yard, and here the Dean and Chapter sent him £5 when he was afflicted with paralysis. He is said to have begged the king's favour for eighteen inches of square ground 'in Westminster Abbey'. In 1637 he died, and was buried in the nave, supposedly in a standing position so as not to exceed his plot. A floor stone now moved to the arcade of the south nave aisle was carved 'O rare Ben Jonson'. It was 'donne at the chardge of Jack Young, afterwards knighted, who, walking here when the grave was covering, gave the fellow eighteen pence to cut it.' In 1849 Dean Buckland resolved to test the tale. When the grave of Sir Robert Wilson was being dug near by, the workmen found a decayed coffin which had been buried in an upright position. Loose sand rippled in, revealing two leg bones bolt upright, and a skull rolling down among the sand, with Jonson's red hair still attached. The fox in his earth.

As King and Parliament, Royalist and Puritan polarised, the fires of an insane fanatical frenzy were fanned. Repressiveness, a lust for destruction, a violent loathing of the old order roamed the streets almost at random. The Abbey, because of its geographical position and association with the monarchy, stood in the front line, and suffered the most serious losses of its entire history. Today's building is only a ghost of that which was humiliated and despoiled by the ugly decade of the 1640s.

There had been a hint of parliamentary hostility as early as 1614, when the Commons chose to receive Communion at St Margaret's rather than the Abbey 'for feare of copes and wafer cakes'. The Puritanical temper of the House drove it to desire common bread rather than the wafer bread of older ritual. As a result, St Margaret's remains still the church favoured by the House of Commons.

But a parliamentary boycott was nothing compared with mob violence. On December 27th 1641, a London mob demonstrated against the bishops on their way to Parliament, and then advanced on the Abbey. "There was a buz among them. Some said "Let us pluck down the organs"; some cried "let us deface the monuments". An

Ben Jonson, poet and dramatist, a pupil at Westminster School, also ended his days in the precinct, and is buried in the nave.

advance guard of apprentices entered the church shouting 'No bishops! No bishops!", but surprisingly left when reproved by a verger. Before the main body arrived, Williams had received warning, and 'made fast the doors, which they found shut against them. When they would have forced them, they were beaten off with stones from the top of the leads' (dropped by officers and scholars of the College), 'the Archbishop all this while maintaining the Abbey in his own person'. After an hour's dispute, when the multitude had been well pelted from aloft, a few of the Archbishop's train opened a door and rushed out with swords drawn, and drove them before them, "like fearful Hares".'

The King who fifteen years earlier had barred Williams from his coronation, approved his resolution: 'My Lord, I commend you that you are no whit daunted with all disasters, but are zealous in defending your order.' 'Please your Majesty, I am a true Welshman, and they are observed never to run away until their general do first forsake them. No fear of my flinching whilst your Majesty doth countenance our cause.'

But these *Boys' Own Paper* heroics could not for long hold back the tidal wave of revolution. In 1642 the bishops were excluded from Parliament, after another attempted charge of high treason which again sent Williams to the Tower. In the same year there was the last meeting of the Chapter before they dispersed to save their skins. In May Williams left London for York, lucky to be alive, never to return. In the abandoned Abbey destruction was king. In 1641 Torrigiano's altar above the tomb of Edward VI was smashed; in 1642 the Long Parliament ordered the removal of the stained glass. Soldiers of the parliamentary army quartered in the church broke up the organ which Williams had defended and pawned its pipes for ale. In 1643 Parliament demanded access to the Regalia. A Mr Martin 'forced open a great Iron Chest, took out the Crowns, the Robes, the Swords and Sceptre belonging anciently to K. Edward the Confessor . . . with a scorne greater than his lusts, and the rest of his vices, he openly declares, "That there would be no further use of those Toys and Trifles . . . with a thousand apish and ridiculous actions exposed those sacred Ornaments to contempt and laughter."' They were all taken to the Tower where, after the King's execution, they were broken up and sold for the weight of the precious metals. All that survived are the spoon made for Henry II or Richard I and the Balas ruby, worn by Henry V at Agincourt, now set in the Imperial State Crown. By 1643

Facing page and above:
The only surviving medallions of 13th-century stained glass, now in the Abbey Museum.

From left to right: St Nicholas *(full page)*; The Stoning of Stephen; The Pentecost; The Massacre of the Innocents; The Ascension; The Martyrdom of St John the Baptist or St Alban.

The Balas ruby, worn by Henry V at the Battle of Agincourt in 1415, is now set in the Imperial State Crown.

The head of Charles I, on the
East Front of St Margaret's
Church, looks across
Old Palace Yard road to . . .

Destruction and miraculous
survival: the elegant alabaster
Weepers (mourners) on the tomb
of John of Eltham, brother of
Edward III, in St Edmund's
Chapel, and . . .

it was too late for peace; a struggle to the death was the only
prospect. Thomas Fuller's Abbey sermon on March 27th, the day of
the King's inauguration, reveals the mistrust that was driving the war
machine. Taking as his text 'My Lord the King is come again in peace
unto his own House', Fuller's words are thunderous and unforgiving.
'Pious princes can take no delight in victories over their subjects. . . .
our sins have made this land drunk with blood. . . . We have cause
to suspect our Peace will not be a true Peace, and an open wound is
better than a palliate cure. Would you have us put off our Armour to
be killed in our clothes?' He is the mouthpiece of civil war in any age.

On November 18th 1645 a new ordinance was published
creating a 'Committee for the College of Westminster', composed of
those who had taken the Covenant. John Bradshaw, later president
of the regicides, took up residence in the Deanery to direct Abbey
affairs. Under the new regime all was changed. Soldiers were on
duty in the church every day to prevent disturbance and suppress dis-
sent at the new style of services. John Vicars rejoices in them: 'Where
as there was wont to be heard, nothing almost but Roaring-Boyes,
tooting and squeaking Organ-Pipes, and the Cathedrall Catches of
Morley, and I know not what trash; now the Popish Altar is quite
taken away, the bellowing Organs are demolisht, the treble, or rather
trouble and base Singers, Chanters, or inchanters, driven out; and
instead thereof, there is now set up a most blessed Orthodox
Preaching Ministry, even every morning through the weeke, and
every weeke through the whole yeare a Sermon Preached by most
learned, grave and godly Ministers . . . and for the gaudy, gilded
Crucifixes, and rotten rabble of dumbe Idols, Popish Saints, and

Pictures where that sinfull singing was used; now a most sweet assembly, and thicke throng of Gods pious people . . . O our God! what a rich and rare alteration! What a strange change is this indeed!' His pamphlet was called 'God's Ark over-topping the World's Waves', but there was not room in his ark for either king or archbishop. Charles was executed in Whitehall on January 29th 1649. His friends wished to bury the body in Henry VII's Chapel, but this was denied them, his enemies conceiving that the sympathies of the people would be too violently moved by so public a funeral. Williams had already fled from York to North Wales, when the parliamentary Hothams sallied out from Hull, threatening to cut off his head. He was prostrated by news of the king's death, which 'pierced the Archbishop's heart with so sharp a point, that sorrow run him down the Hill with that violence, that he never stayed till he came to the bottom, and died', on March 25th 1650. His tomb stands in the little church at Llandegai, near Caernarvon. 'He tasted equally of great Prosperity and Adversity,' wrote the faithful Hacket, 'and was a rare example in both.'

. . . Oliver Cromwell, standing in front of Westminster Hall, in the Palace of Westminster.

With the king's death, the storm seemed to spend itself. 'President Bradshaw' haunted the Abbey in life, as he is said to do still as a ghost, ordering a quiet room to be built for him at triforium level in the south-west tower, where he died in 1659, a year after Cromwell. In 'the Chair of Scotland' conveyed from the Abbey to Westminster Hall, Cromwell had been 'crowned' Lord Protector in 1657. In September 1658 he died, and his funeral took place about two months later, on November 23rd, at night. John Evelyn describes 'Oliver lying in Effigie in royal robes, and crown'd with a Crown,

. . . their battered counterparts on the tomb of Aveline, Countess of Lancaster, in the Sacrarium.

scepter and like a King. It was the joyfullest funerall that ever I saw, for there was none that cried, but dogs, which the soldiers hooted away with a barbarous noise; drinking, and taking Tabacco in the streets as they went.' His hearse was lodged in Henry VII's Chapel, and the monument keepers made a good profit from visitors for some months. And with Cromwell the visionary social, political and ecclesiastical adventure, already fading, lost its last brightness leaving behind much wreckage and little fondness. Cromwell may have had the last laugh, though. There were witnesses to a story that, anticipating the restoration of the monarchy, he had ordered his own burial in anonymity, on the Naseby battlefield, and that in the coffin buried in the Abbey were substituted the remains of Charles I. So when the bodies of the regicides were dug up and heads spiked in mockery at Westminster Hall in January 1661, it would have been a royal head that was reviled.

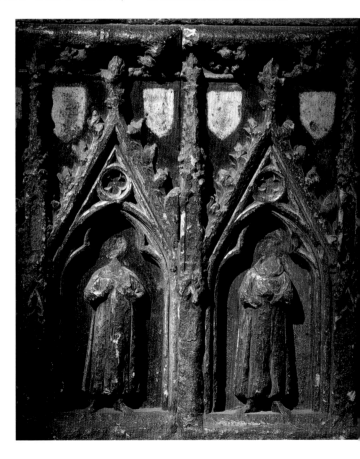

The Hanoverian Coat of Arms on Hawksmoor's West Front, which was completed in the 1740s.

Order Restored

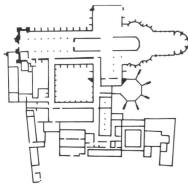

Blue: Nicholas Hawksmoor's new West Towers
Pale blue: Renovation of north end of North Transept by Sir Christopher Wren

Oliver Cromwell, Lord Protector after the execution of Charles I in 1649, was buried in Henry VII's Chapel when he died in 1658. But after the Restoration his body was dug up, hanged on the gallows at Tyburn (now Marble Arch), and thrown anonymously into a pit.

The first months of the restored monarchy were tentative ones. There had been too much fear, loss, suffering for the trauma to pass easily away, despite the festivity which greeted Charles II on May 29th 1660 as he returned to his capital. People in London seemed to creep about in a limbo between two political orders, the one not yet buried and the other not yet born. Samuel Pepys, a resident at this time in Axe Yard, off King Street (now Whitehall), was often at the Abbey. In October he reports a thin congregation for a service attended by several bishops, who were in the Abbey for the first time since, under the Long Parliament, the Assembly of Divines had met in Henry VII's Chapel to debate the 'extirpation of prelacy'. Their return met with no enthusiasm: 'But Lord, at their going out, how people did most of them look upon them as strange Creatures, and few with any kind of love or Respect.' In November Pepys records 'the very first time that ever I heard the organs in a Cathedral'. He was an enthusiastic amateur musician, and was pleased, in December 1661, when Mr Hooper took him in among the Quire, where he sang with them at their service. He was disquieted, however, by the treatment of the bodies of the Cromwellians after the Restoration. Some had been thrown into a common pit in St Margaret's Churchyard, by the back door of the house that had been William Laud's when he was a prebendary. On January 30th 1661, the twelfth anniversary of the king's execution, Pepys's fellow-diarist John Evelyn chronicles a further outrage: 'This day were the Carkasses of that arch-rebel Cromwell, Bradshaw the Judge who condemn'd his Majestie and Ireton . . . dragged out of their superbe Tombs (in Westminster among the Kings), to Tyburne, and hanged on the gallows there from 9 in the morning til 6 at night, and then buried under that fatal and ignominious Monument in a deepe pitt.' Pepys's comment is less triumphalist: it troubles him 'that a man of so great courage as Cromwell was should have that dishonour, though otherwise he might deserve it enough'.

Charles II's English coronation (the Scots had crowned him at Scone on New Year's Day 1651) on St George's Day, April 23rd 1661, brought to a close the uneasy transition from Commonwealth to

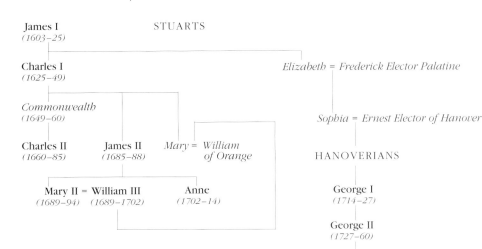

Effigy of Charles II, made for his funeral in 1685, and now in the Abbey Museum.

STUARTS

James I
(1603–25)

Charles I
(1625–49)

Elizabeth = Frederick Elector Palatine

Commonwealth
(1649–60)

Sophia = Ernest Elector of Hanover

Charles II   James II   *Mary = William*
(1660–85)   *(1685–88)*   *of Orange*

HANOVERIANS

Mary II = William III   Anne
(1689–94) *(1689–1702)*   *(1702–14)*

George I
(1714–27)

George II
(1727–60)

Frederick

George III
(1760–1820)

monarchy. The persistent Pepys was there, having made an early start: 'With much ado . . . did get up into a great scaffold across the north end of the abbey where with a great deal of patience I sat from past 4 till 11 before the King came in . . . so great a noise, that I could make but little of the Musique.' The diarist's patience was stronger than his bladder, however: 'But I had so great a list to pisse, that I went out a little while before the King had done all his ceremonies.' Other calls of nature took Pepys to the Abbey in the next few years: 'Found Jane at my barber's—got the poor wretch to promise to meet me in the abby on tomorrow come sennit . . . but no Jane came, which vexed me.' Next week, he waited all afternoon in the Cloister, 'but she came not'. But at last his sacred rendezvous proved satisfactory: he made an assignation with Mrs Burroughs at the west door 'where she came to me'.

Peter Heylyn, Laud's chaplain and thorn in the flesh of Dean Williams, had survived the Commonwealth the hard way. His house was stripped, his library dispersed, his family broken up, and he himself driven for seventeen years to vagrancy and disguise in order to elude capture. A worn and broken man, he returned to Westminster as Sub-Dean in 1660, and took part in Charles II's coronation. A month later, on the first anniversary of the Restoration, his sermon polarised and released his tumultuous feelings. It hinged on the conceit that Charles was a latter-day David (was this the origin of Dryden's analogies in Absalom and Achitophel?) and paid thankfulness to God for 'giving us such a fair and blessed sun-shine after a long Egyptian darkness'. His peroration exploited the contrast between then and now. Under the Commonwealth, 'No news in any of our Streets, but that of leading men into fresh captivity; nor Musick to be heard in our private Houses, but the sighs, groans, and cries of afflicted people, . . . our persons haled into the prisons, and our heads to the block, our children born to bondage, and brought up to servitude, our goods taken from us, and exposed to sale . . . such a confusion in the City, such spoils and rapines in the Countrey, and such oppressions in all places under their command; that greater miseries never fell upon God's own people in those wretched times, in which there was no King in Israel.' But now, 'what pen is able to express the Triumphs of those two great dayes, when all the bravery of the

1660 The Restoration

April 23rd 1661
Coronation of Charles II

1674 Discovery in the Tower of London of bones thought to be those of the princes murdered in 1483; reinterment in the Abbey

April 23rd 1685
Coronation of James II

1688 Deposition of James II

April 11th 1689 Coronation of William III and Mary II

March 5th 1695
Burial of Mary II

November 26th 1695 Burial of Henry Purcell, *Organist*

1698
Christopher Wren, *Surveyor*

April 24th 1702
Coronation of Anne

1713 Francis Atterbury, *Dean*

October 20th 1714
Coronation of George I

August 24th 1723
Arrest of Atterbury

October 11th 1727
Coronation of George II

1745 West Towers completed

April 20th 1759
Burial of Handel

November 11th 1760
George II, last monarch buried in the Abbey

1776 James Wyatt, *Surveyor*

December 20th 1784
Burial of Samuel Johnson

June 1st 1791
Joseph Haydn present at Handel commemoration.

Nation seemed to be powred into the City, and the whole City
emptied into some few streets, the windows in those street to be glased
with eyes, the houses in a manner to be tyled with men; and all the
peple in the streets, the windowes and the house tops also, ingeminat-
ing and regeminating this most joyful acclamation, God save the King.'

But the effusion of greeting for a restored king seemed to
spend itself in one great sigh of relief, and leave the citizens bankrupt
of enthusiasm for their monarchs for over two centuries. At
Westminster there were to be no more scenes of popular rejoicing
until Queen Victoria's Golden Jubilee in 1887. Three last Stuarts and
five Hanoverians failed to win their subjects' hearts; only Mary II was
popularly mourned as the daughter of James II. Apart from the grand
rituals of coronations and, until 1760, funerals, the politically emascu-
lated royal house furnishes only footnotes to the history of the Abbey
in the 18th century. They are displaced in the picture by great subjects—politicians, warriors, artists, and scores of lesser men and
women who sought the consolation of immortal greatness in Abbey
tomb or memorial—and by visitors, domestic and foreign, whom
curiosity drew to Westminster, and whose reactions often display a
sceptical or irreverent temper, the magic of monarchy and church
being largely in abeyance.

Charles II was buried on February 13th 1685, at night, very
obscurely, in a vault under Henry VII's Chapel, 'without any manner
of pomp, and soone forgotten after all this vainity, and the face of the
whole Court exceedingly changed into a more solemne and moral
behaviour; the new King affecting neither Prophanesse, nor buffoon-
ery.' During the preparations for James II's coronation, a falling plank
gashed a hole in the chest containing the body of Edward the
Confessor. A quireman reached in and took out the Saint's crucifix
and chain, and also drew the head to the aperture to view it. The
treasure was passed to the king down a notable line of Archbishop
(York), Archbishop (Canterbury) and Dean of Westminster, a hierarchy to which many a dean would drink a toast. James gave the thief
a bounty, and the jewel was never seen again, though many have
sought to trace it. It was listed in the inventory of the possessions of
Mary of Modena, James's wife, at her death in 1718, and was presented to Pope Benedict XIII in 1729 by the Young Pretender. It has
never yet surfaced in the Vatican. The theft of the Confessor's treasure seemed to have placed a curse on the subsequent coronation.
The crown was not well fitted, came down too far, and covered the
upper part of James's face. At one moment it tottered on his head;
Henry Sidney, Keeper of the Robes, steadied it with the words, 'This
is not the first time our family has supported the crown'. The canopy
held over the king suddenly and inexplicably tore: 'Twas of cloth of
gold,' noted John Aubrey, '(and my strength could not, I am confident,
have rent it), and it was not a windy day.' Also torn was the flag flying from the White Tower. His bastard son by Mrs Sidley died on that
same day. So the end of his brief reign, during which the country
(except for those trimmers who changed their faith promptly on the
king's accession) felt menaced by the prospect of a second return to

Some of the Abbey choristers
in the coronation procession
of James II in 1685.

Roman Catholicism, was augured at its very beginning. After his flight abroad in 1688, constitutional order was assured by the coronation of William of Orange and Mary Stuart as joint monarchs, William III and Mary II. Their coronation in 1689 was delayed for two hours by the news of James II's landing in Ireland. The short king and tall queen, crowned in a copy of the Coronation Chair made for the occasion, cut an incongruous pair of figures. William's purse was stolen from his side during the ceremony, and he had no money for the offertory; Princess Anne, at the queen's side, observed at one juncture, 'Madam, I pity your fatigue.' Mary's tart reply, 'A crown, sister, is not so heavy as it seems', was to echo unkindly when Anne herself was crowned thirteen years later at the age of 37. The combination of gout and corpulence meant that she had to be carried or lifted in a low armchair and supported at every stage of the ceremony. Small wonder, amid such scenes, that the allure of monarchy was in decline.

But Mary's death, in December 1694, of smallpox, aroused genuine grief. Even allowing for the hyperbole by which eye-witnesses confer importance on themselves,

Mary II's death in 1694 caused widespread grief. Her funeral in March 1695 was a sumptuous one, with music written by Henry Purcell, organist of the Abbey, who was himself to die prematurely in 1695.

The memorial tablet to Henry Purcell placed on a pillar in the North Quire Aisle in 1695.

Samuel Pepys, whose diary contains many references to events within the Abbey, took part in the coronation procession of King James II in 1685 as a Warden of the Cinque Ports. He is thought to be the fat-faced man supporting the canopy at the front, nearest the viewer.

the scenes at her funeral appear to have had few rivals for melancholy pageantry. It was intensely cold; the Thames had been frozen over since January, and a snowstorm beset the long procession on March 5th 'so that the Ladies had but draggled trains by the time they got thither'. Evelyn grumbled at the cost (about £50,000, he alleged), but adds 'Was the Queen's funeral infinitely expensive, never so universal a mourning, all the Parliament men had cloaks given them, and also 400 poore women, all the streets hung, and the middle of the streets boarded and covered with black cloth.' In the Abbey her body was placed under a black velvet canopy fringed with silver, around it hundreds of candles blazing. Purcell's funeral music, of stark grandeur, sounded the heroic strain; a frozen robin, said to have perched on the hearse throughout, the pathetic. The guns from the distant Tower, firing every minute during the service, echoed leadenly against the heavy sky.

The Abbey organist, Henry Purcell, was already ill, and the intense cold of the day gave him a chill which hastened his own death in the November following. He was a Westminster child, born, probably, on the south side of the Great Almonry. His father, Henry senior, was organist before him, and at his sudden death in 1664 was buried in the East Cloister. Young Henry, who had worked in the Abbey as a boy, copying music and tuning the organ, and whose genius may have been recognised and supported by the redoubtable Richard Busby, Prebendary and Head Master of Westminster School (as had the talents of Christopher Wren and Robert Hooke) was appointed organist of Westminster Abbey in 1679, at the age of 20, at a salary of £10 per annum. John Blow, his predecessor, and eventual successor, modestly made way for a young man so gifted. For sixteen more years his prodigious talent flowered, at Westminster, at the Chapel Royal, at the court, in the theatre, in popular music making, and in bawdy tavern songs. Though involved in a spat with the Dean and Chapter over the sale of places in the organ loft at the coronation in 1689 (it was a common practice in the late 17th century for the Dean and Chapter on great occasions to divide the spoils accruing from spectators seated both inside the Abbey and on scaffolds outside it), he retained his position, and his proper share of the profits, only to die of consumption on November 21st 1695, at the age of 36. The *Post Boy* journal for November 28th reported that 'Dr Purcel was Interred at Westminster on Tuesday night in a magnificent manner. He is much lamented, being a very great Master of Musick.' His funeral music for Queen Mary sounded again for himself when he was buried in the North Quire Aisle, proof enough in itself of the eulogy on his nearby memorial, that 'he is gone to that blessed place where only his harmony can be exceeded.' Purcell's genius adorned the services, Wren's was called upon to preserve the fabric. For the building was starting to show its age. Pepys was alarmed in 1660 when 'in the middst of sermon some plaster fell from the topp of the Abbey, that made me and all the rest in our pew afeard, and I wished myself out.' Neglect during the years of trouble, the English weather, and the burning of sea-coal were the villains. John Evelyn had inveighed against sea-coal in 1661: 'It is this horrid smoak which obscures our Churches, and makes our Palaces look old, which fouls our Clothes, and corrupts the waters . . . It is this which scatters and strews about those black and smutty atomes upon all things . . . .' Wren was appointed Surveyor of the Fabric in 1698. His report to the Dean and Chapter made grim reading. Stone is decayed four inches deep and falls off perpetually in great scales. Henry VII's Chapel, derided by Evelyn as 'crinkle crankle' by the standards of Wren's St Paul's and Inigo Jones's Banqueting House, was approved by Wren himself as 'a nice embroidered work and tho' lately built in comparison, is so eaten up by our weather, that it begs for some compassion.' Wren directed the repair of large parts of the fabric, though he was impeded by the houses still abutting against the walls on the north side. He strengthened the crossing tower with tie-bars, and contemplated a central spire, the model for which is still displayed in the North Transept. The cost of his work was partly funded by the earliest, though unintended, example of environmental legislation: a portion of the duty on coal was assigned to the fabric of St Paul's and Westminster Abbey. The polluter properly paid.

In 1713 Francis Atterbury was installed as Dean of Westminster. He was to be the Dean of the century, as Williams had been before him, and Stanley after him. Educated at Westminster and devoted to the interests of the School, a fine orator, a Tory and man

Henry VII's Chapel, derided by John Evelyn the diarist as 'crinkle crankle', but praised by Wren as 'a nice embroidered work', needed major repairs by Wren, Wyatt (1809–22) and again in the 1990s.

That 'very great Master of Musick'. Each Abbey organist, since the 16th century, is remembered in the panes that surround this 20th-century memorial to Purcell in the Choir School.

Sir Isaac Newton (1642–1727) was buried in the Abbey, and his monument stands on the north side of the Organ Screen gate. Voltaire was among the mourners at his funeral.

of letters, close friend of Swift and Pope, he was a great man, and would have been greater still but for the unfortunate timing of the succession in 1714, which brought George I from Hanover to be crowned at Westminster. On the death of Queen Anne, the impulsive Atterbury proposed to proclaim the Stuart Pretender as king. He was a member of a Jacobite Cabal from 1715, and was in regular correspondence with Charles Stuart. 'My daily prayer to God', he wrote to him in 1717, 'is that you may have success in the Just Cause wherein you are engaged.' His letter of 1721 encouraging an invasion fell into the hands of Sir Robert Walpole, who tried unsuccessfully to buy his loyalty. At this crisis in his fortunes, ensnared in politics, resigned to failure, he finds comfort in friendship, and writes to Alexander Pope in April 1722: 'I am at this moment building a vault in the Abbey for me and mine. It was to be in the Abbey, because of my relation to the place; but it is at the West door of it, as far from Kings and Kaesars as the space will admit of.'

In August he was arrested at the Deanery. 'He desired they would let his servant shave him before they carried him off, but that was not allowed.' He was sent that same day to the Tower, where he suffered nine months of rigorous imprisonment. 'I have been treated with such severity and so great indignity as I believe no prisoner in the Tower of my age, infirmities, position, and rank ever underwent.' 'How shin'd the Soul, unconquered in the Tower,' ran Pope's tribute to his friend. He was a popular churchman, and Walpole, fearing riots, orchestrated a pamphlet war against him. Writers and publishers of squibs in his defence were taken into custody. In 1723 a parliamentary Bill of Pains and Penalties against him was passed by 83 votes to 43, and in June he was exiled, denied leave to pay a last visit to the Abbey before embarking on a man-of-war at Woolwich. He died in Paris in March 1732, and was buried at Westminster in May in the vault which he had prepared. Though actresses such as Anne Oldfield were honoured by a lying-in-state in the Jerusalem Chamber, Francis Atterbury's coffin was laid out for one day in the workmen's lumber-room. His voice rings defiantly from the grave, in the Latin epitaph he wrote as his own apologia. An English version of its conclusion runs: 'Posterity, beware! That man Robert Walpole resolved upon, undertook, and committed this crime (helped especially by the votes of the bishops) — and all posterity will know him.'

After Atterbury, there is little evidence of either dynamism or quality among the Deans and Prebendaries of Westminster. It was possible for them to make a comfortable living for comparatively little exertion. Many divided their time between the Abbey and country livings; all benefited from the systematising of the 17th-century practice of sharing out fees from services, especially funerals. So the sale of space in the Abbey was irresistibly tempting, and rich but dissolute figures were welcomed in: Thomas Thynne, for example, wealthy

and wanton, after his assassination in his coach in Pall
Mall by hired killers, as a result of a complex and dis-
creditable romantic intrigue in which, as it was said of
him, he would neither sleep with his wife nor marry his
mistress. Dean Sprat ordered the removal of a fulsome
epitaph from his monument on the grounds of its
untruthfulness. A substantial monument in the Nave to
Mrs Katharine Bovey, not even buried at Westminster,
praises her because 'the great share of time allowed to
the closet was not perceived in her Œconomy'. A
decent virtue, no doubt, but a dubious qualification for
a place in the National Pantheon. When Dean Pearce

Thomas Thynne, assassinated in
his carriage in St James's in 1682
was so notorious a rogue that
Dean Sprat later ordered the
obliteration of parts of the
inscription on the tomb in the
South Quire aisle on the ground
of their untruthfulness.

seemed on the point of consenting to the removal of the medieval
tomb of Aymer de Valence in order to make way for General Wolfe,
it took the outrage of Horace Walpole to dissuade him. Walpole
writes a despairing letter to a friend: 'The chapter of Westminster sell
their church over and over again; the ancient monuments tumble
upon one's head through their neglect, as one of them did, and killed
a man at Lady Elizabeth Percy's funeral; and they erect new waxen
dolls of queen Elizabeth etc to draw visits and money from the mob.'
Though charges for services were intended to furnish the Fabric
Fund, there was clearly little over once the hands of all and sundry
had dipped into the coffer. From 1730 such building funds as were
available were applied to the last major construction project in the
Abbey's history, the completion of Nicholas Hawksmoor's design for
the West Towers, left oddly truncated and unbalanced in 1500. The
Dean and Chapter were not absolutely uncharitable—five pounds

The effigy on the late 13th-century
tomb of William de Valence in
the Chapel of St Edmund.
William was the father of Aymer
de Valence, and half-brother
of Henry III.

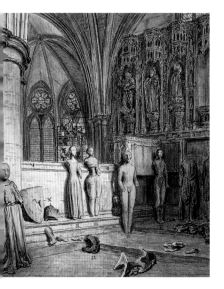

'The Ragged Regiment', drawn by John Carter in 1786. The effigies from royal and noble funerals were the prerequisites of first the Abbot and monastery, and later the Dean and Chapter. Though they have often attracted visitors, they have also proved awkward company to house and display.

Mid-18th century map of Westminster.

was awarded in 1735 to a poor labouring man who had received hurt in one of his hands as he was working at the West Tower—but there is little evidence of their sense of responsibility either for Westminster's medieval treasures or for suffering humanity. In 1750 a beadle is appointed to keep the Abbey and Cloisters and Dean's Yard free from vagrants and beggars 'with which we are horribly pestered'; in the same year Prebendary Thomas Wilson records in his diary for April 17th: 'Preached at the Abbey. Went to St Paules. Heard the Bishop of Worcester against the Idleness of the Poor and their drinking of gin. An admirable sermon. Dined at Dolleys.' Much of the fabric, inside and out, was in disrepair. Statues were removed from the exterior of Henry VII's Chapel lest they should fall on the heads of those who attended the Parliament; in 1723 it was recorded that the shields had been torn away from Richard II's tomb, leaving holes in it. Nothing had been done by 1766 when Gerard Andrewes, a Westminster scholar, later Dean of Canterbury, saw another boy reach a hand in and take out the royal jawbone. He thrashed the boy, and took the bone for himself. It passed down as a relic in his family until 1906, when it was restored to the tomb. In 1776 James Wyatt, Surveyor of the Fabric, was permitted to remove and make a bonfire of the medieval choir stalls.

Under such ramshackle stewardship it is no surprise that many of the great events of the period were more than usually mismanaged, sometimes with a destructiveness that rivalled through accident and indifference the more systematic depredations under the Commonwealth. George I, summoned from Germany to be crowned in 1714, spoke no English; popular feeling was tepid and there was

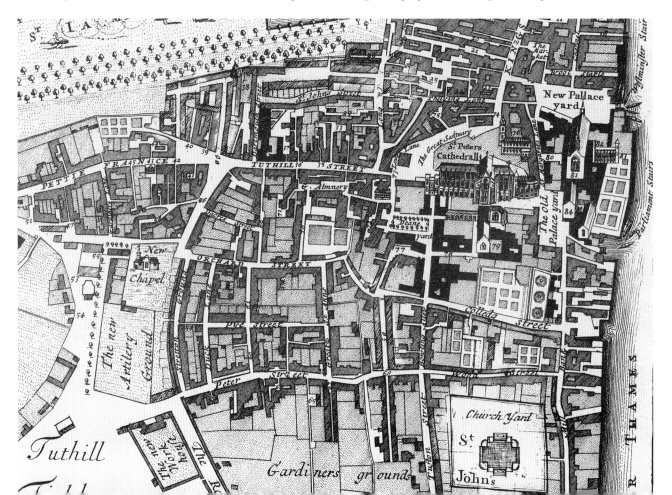

much anxiety about possible displays of Jacobite sentiment. The ceremony had to be explained to him in broken Latin, prompting a popular jest that much bad language had been uttered in the service. At one point he rudely rejected Atterbury's offer of the canopy; what on earth might he have imagined it was for?

In 1727 George II and Queen Caroline were crowned. It was the occasion of the first performance of Handel's Coronation Anthems, of which Zadok the Priest has since been heard at every subsequent ceremony. Lord Hervey, who was present, was torn between realism and sycophancy: 'His Majesty, despite his low stature and fair hair, which heightened the meekness of his expression at this period, was, on this occasion, every inch a king.' At his death in 1760, George II's was the last burial of a monarch at Westminster. Horace Walpole's account of it, in a letter to George Montagu, though a well-known anthology piece, gives an indispensable picture of the age. It is a scene in every way worthy of Vanburgh or Congreve: 'Do you know, I had the curiosity to go to the burying t'other night; I had never seen a royal funeral . . . the charm was the entrance of the abbey, where we were received by the dean and chapter in rich robes, the choir and almsmen bearing torches; the whole abbey so illuminated, that one saw it to greater advantage than by day . . . When we came to the chapel of Henry the Seventh, all solemnity and decorum ceased; no order was observed, people sat or stood where they could or would. The yeoman of the guard were crying out for help, oppressed by the immense weight of the coffin; the bishop read sadly and blundered in the prayers; . . . and the

Handel's monument on the west wall of the South Transept.

A fantasy painting by Pietro Fabris (c. 1735) showing the north profile as it might have appeared if the dreams of Wren and Hawksmoor in the early 18th century had been realised.

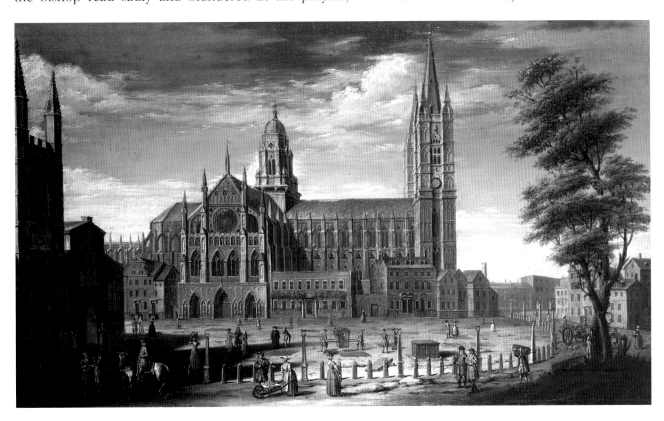

Old Palace Yard by Thomas Malton Jr. in 1796.

Dean's Yard c.1790–1800: many of the old monastic farm buildings survived in a higgledy-piggledy fashion until 1815, when the present Dean's Yard was laid out.

anthem . . . would have served as well for a nuptial. The real serious part was the figure of the duke of Cumberland . . . attending the funeral of a father could not be pleasant: his leg extremely bad, yet forced to stand upon it near two hours; his face bloated and distorted with his late paralytic stroke . . . and placed over the mouth of the vault, into which, in all probability, he must himself so soon descend; think how unpleasant a situation! He bore it all with a firm and unaffected countenance. This grave scene was fully contrasted by the burlesque Duke of Newcastle. He fell into a fit of crying the moment he came into the chapel and flung himself back in a stall, the archbishop hovering over him with a smelling-bottle; but in two minutes his curiosity got the better of his hypocrisy, and he ran about the chapel with his glass to spy who was or was not there, spying with one hand and mopping his eyes with the other. Then returned the fear of catching cold; and the Duke of Cumberland, who was sinking with the heat, felt himself weighed down, and turning round, found it was the Duke of Newcastle standing upon his train, to avoid the chill of the marble. It was very theatric to look down into the vault, where the coffin lay, attended by mourners with lights.'

George III's Coronation in 1761 was a muddle. The procession left Westminster Hall one and a half hours late, and it was dusk before king and queen left the Abbey. The tradition of irreverence at 18th-century coronations was extended: there were cheers and jeers for opposing politicians like those of a football crowd; there was a ferocious scrambling for medals as they were scattered among the congregation, and when the Archbishop ascended into the pulpit for the sermon, the crowd took that opportunity to eat their meal, when the general clattering of knives, forks, plates and glasses that ensued, produced a most ridiculous effect, and a universal burst of laughter followed. The egregious Duke of Newcastle again distinguished himself. The Queen had a retiring chamber, with all the conveniences prepared behind the altar. She went thither—in the most convenient, what found she but—the Duke of Newcastle. 'Well! It was all delightful,' reflected Horace Walpole, 'but not half so charming as its being over. Puppet show it was, though it cost a million.' There speaks a modern voice.

The plain Purbeck marble tomb of Edward I was again the object of unwelcome attention in 1774, when it was opened out of curiosity. A coffin of varnished Purbeck marble, 6 ft. 7 in. long contained the corpse, 'richly habited and almost intire'. The body, 6 ft. 2 in. long, had been wrapped in cerecloth to preserve it. Mr Gough saw a 'visage so well preserved as to exhibit a likeness to an able Draughtsman . . . his hands bare and entire (bone with a dry tanned skin, but no nails)'. At this point he was beset by covetousness. Another eye-witness takes up the tale: 'Mr G was observed to put his hand into the Coffin and immediately to apply it to his pocket; but not so dexterously, but that the Dean of Westminster saw it: he remonstrated against the propriety of it, and Mr Gough denying the fact, the Dean insisted on the Pocket being searched: where they found that he had taken a finger; which was replaced. I cannot tell how to believe it'.

A young draughtsman's apprentice had been assigned that same year, when he was 16, to sketch monuments in the Abbey for engravings for Richard Gough's 'Sepulchral Monuments'. It is pos-

The Argyll monument in the South Transept at sunrise.

Epstein's head of William Blake in Poets' Corner broods over the building where the young visionary's imagination was aroused.

sible that he was present at the opening of Edward I's tomb, to make drawings of the scene (which are now in the care of the Society of Antiquaries). William Blake wrote to Samuel Palmer later in his life that 'in Westminster Abbey were his earliest and most sacred recollections'. He studied the tomb effigies intensely, 'in every point he could catch, frequently standing on the monument and viewing the figures from the top'. Here one day a Westminster boy, having already tormented him, got up to some pinnacle level with his platform the better to annoy him. In the impetuosity of

his anger Blake dislodged him and precipitated him to the ground on which he fell with terrific violence. Blake was captivated by the Abbey. Although the medieval colour was fading, there was still some paintwork on stone and wood: the Ancient of Days on Richard II's tomb canopy, the intensity of colour in the surviving stained glass and the elongated figures on the tombs were among the features which baptised his impressionable imagination with medieval Gothic. It was here too that his visionary powers were nurtured. Palmer reported Blake's remembrance: 'The aisles and galleries of the old cathedral suddenly filled with a great procession of monks and priests, choristers and censer bearers, and his entranced ears heard the chant of plainsong and chorale, while the vaulted roof trembled to the sound of organ music.'

A much more senior man of letters, a devout Anglican and frequent visitor to the Abbey precinct at this period, Samuel Johnson, 'who would never consent to disgrace the walls of Westminster Abbey with an English inscription' took his delights very differently from the young Blake. Dean Zachary Pearce assisted him with his *Dictionary*, and Dr John Taylor, a prebendary living in Little Dean's Yard, was one of his dearest friends, even

The elongated figures of the Abbey, sculpted and painted, impressed themselves on the eye of William Blake, and shaped his own draughtsmanship.

A barley twist column, at a corner of Edward the Confessor's Shrine, glowing with fragments of Cosmati work still in place.

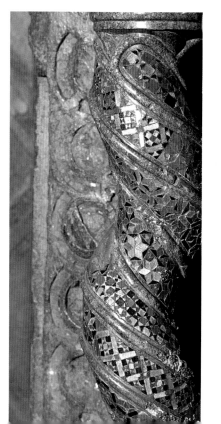

though Johnson humorously complained that 'his talk is mainly of bullocks', and that his habit of going to bed very early was 'very disagreeable to a man who likes to fold his legs and have his talk out, as I do'. Johnson was present in Poets' Corner in 1779 when the friend of his youth from Lichfield, David Garrick, with whom he had first travelled to London, was given a funeral on a royal scale. Peers carried the pall; Reynolds, Burke, Gibbon, and all the players from Covent Garden and Drury Lane watched Garrick's coffin lowered into the grave at the foot of the monument to Shakespeare, where Johnson stood bathed in tears.

Five years later, on December 20th 1784, Johnson himself was buried near Garrick, but his funeral was austere. Charles Burney senior explains in a letter to Thomas Twining that Johnson's executor was to blame: 'The Dean and Chapter of Westminster Abbey lay all the blame on Sir John Hawkins for suffering Johnson to be so unworthily interred. The Knight's first inquiry at the Abbey . . . was— "What would be the difference in the expense between a public and a private funeral?" and he was told only a few pounds to the prebendaries and about ninety pairs of gloves to the choir and attendants; and he then determined that, 'as Dr Johnson had no music in him, he should choose the cheapest manner of interment".' Burney's son, another Charles, who was also present, displays much more youthful intemperance in a letter to Dr Parr: 'Sir John Hawkins did not manage things well, for there was no anthem, or choir service performed—no lesson—but merely what is read over every old woman that is buried by the parish. Surely, surely, my dear Sir, this was wrong, very wrong. Dr Taylor read the service—but so-so.' Parr was inclined to blame the

Chapter; the mutilated service 'is a great reproach to the lazy cattle who loll in the stalls there.'

Johnson's plain burial is matched by a simple monument, Garrick's extravagant one by a flamboyant image of the actor taking his final bow. Above Johnson's tomb slab, and in contrast to the prancing Garrick on the transept arcading, is Roubiliac's monument to Handel, a figure of portly worth. His funeral in 1759, though a private one, had drawn three thousand mourners. On the 25th anniversary of his death, in 1784, he was commemorated by a grand concert of his music in the Nave, the forerunner of others over the next seven years. The first series of concerts ever to be held in the Abbey was also the first to be given to raise money for two charities: £1,000 for Westminster Hospital, and £6,000 for the Society for Decayed Musicians. A choir of nearly three hundred and an orchestra only slightly smaller must have made it an astonishing event for the audience, once they were able to gain access to the church. The Abbey was besieged by an eager public on a hot day in May; the gates, advertised to be open at 9 in the morning, remained closed until 10. There were chaotic scenes in the mêlée: women screamed and fainted, men threatened to break down the doors. Charles Burney's account limits the mischief to 'dishevelled hair and torn garments'; Parker's *General Advertiser* and *Morning Intelligencer* next day was much more censorious: 'Above one hundred persons overcome by the Calcuttean heat which naturally arose from the effluvia of so many close packed bodies, fainted away, [some] were taken home with very little hopes of recovery . . . there certainly has never been in this country a meeting from which so much injury to the health has and will arise, and which in future must bring down so many curses on its authors from parents for the loss of children, and children for the loss of parents . . . the general expression when the concert ended was "I would not undergo such another purgatory to hear even Handel himself—and I am sure I feel myself but ill, very ill paid for what I have suffered."'

But this jeremiad went unheeded: the king and queen entered the royal box at midday, and their pleasure and astonishment at the spectacle were visible to their delighted subjects present. 'Zadok the Priest' as a processional symphony triumphantly launched a concert which gave such satisfaction that the precedent was repeated in each of the next three years, and in 1791, when George III again gave it his patronage. On this occasion the king rose to his feet at the opening chords of the Hallelujah Chorus, prompting the entire audience to follow him. 'Not an eye remained dry.' Haydn, then on a visit to London, was standing near the royal box, and wept like a child, exclaiming—'He is the greatest of us all.' The chief guest at a revival of the Handel concerts in 1834 was less possessed by the music. During a performance of 'Israel in Egypt', William IV fell asleep. Queen Adelaide, seeking to stir him, tapped his arm and

David Garrick takes his final curtain call on his monument in the South Transept.

A monument to William Shakespeare, erected in 1740 through the efforts of David Garrick, instituted the tradition of commemorating writers who were buried elsewhere.

observed: 'What a beautiful duet: "The Lord is a Man of War".' The nautical King, only half-awake, started up and exclaimed in a loud voice: 'Man of War, Man of War—how many guns, how many guns?'

Madman, fop, dullard: the English clung on to their three last Hanoverian kings. It was a tribute to the restored order of the 17th century, embodied in the Act of Settlement of 1689 and its associated legislation, the Bill of Rights and the Habeas Corpus Act, that the upheavals of the Commonwealth had not been repeated, despite the power of Jacobite feeling, the succession of unappealing monarchs and the dissemination of radical political and social doctrines. The House of Lords had continued to regard the Abbey as its official church when the Commons had selected St Margaret's in 1614. Until nearly the end of the 19th century, it was customary for the peers to attend a service there each January 30th, the anniversary of Charles I's execution. In 1793 news of the execution of Louis XVI in France had reached London a few days before, and the city was in ferment. Samuel Horsley, Bishop of St David's, had been selected to preach, and seized the opportunity to deliver one of the most highly charged sermons the Abbey has ever heard, and one which curiously parallels Heylyn's Restoration sermon of 1661 with which this chapter opened. Towards the end, Horsley linked the English regicides of 1649 with the French regicides of 1793, reminding his congregation that the French had found their precedent in England, but extolling the good sense and liberty of dispute which the English political settlement, 'a finished perfection' had fostered. The Lords at this point rose to their feet and remained standing to the end, as an impassioned Horsley cited 'The horrible example which the present hour exhibits, in the unparalleled misery of a neighbouring nation, once great in learning, arts and arms,

now torn by contending factions; her government demolished — her altars overthrown — her first born despoiled of their birth-right — her nobles degraded — her best citizens exiled — her riches, sacred and prophane, given up to the pillage of sacrilege and rapine — atheists directing her councils — desperadoes conducting her armies — war of unjust and chimerical ambition consuming her youth — her granaries exhausted — her fields uncultivated — famine threatening her multitudes — her streets swarming with assassins, filled with violence, deluged with blood! . . . O my country! read the horror of thy own deed in this recent heightened imitation! Lament and weep that this black French treason should have found its example in the crime of thy unnatural sons! Our contrition for our guilt that stained our land . . . will be best expressed by us all by setting the example of a dutiful submission to government in our own conduct, and by inculcating upon our children and dependants a loyal attachment to a king who hath ever sought his own glory in the virtue and prosperity of his people, and administers justice with an even, firm and gentle hand.'

  Horsley's complacent *schadenfreude* provides an intelligible context for the popular heroism of Nelson and Wellington in the French wars that lie just ahead, but rests on assumptions of a settled social order ill-suited to meet the shock of industrial change and its redrawing of the demographic map on identifiably modern lines. The metropolis was about to be transformed, as in our day the cities of the Third World have been, by tidal waves of the rural poor seeking work and fortune. It was to take the Dean and Chapter over fifty years to adjust to the change.

Canaletto's view of Westminster from Lambeth in 1746.

Charles Barry's memorial brass in the Nave.

George III
(1760–1820)   HANOVERIANS

George IV   William IV   *Edward*
(1820–30)   *(1830–37)*   *Duke of Kent*

Victoria
(1837–1901)

The Old
Order Changeth

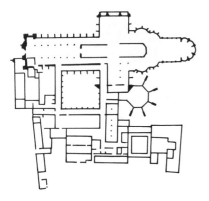

Major renovations by,
pale blue: James Wyatt,
blue: Sir George Gilbert Scott

The West Towers and Broad
Sanctuary about 1880: no trees,
no traffic, no tourists.

Travellers, later torrential, first began to trickle into Westminster in the 18th century. English essayists brought notice of the Abbey to a reading public; improvement in roads brought a wide range of the curious and self-improving from home and abroad. By 1842, when the concentration of people in the metropolis and the beginnings of a railway system were creating new opportunities for visitors, there were about 90,000 sightseers a year entering the place. The foot of tourism was already firmly in the door.

But the reactions of many early tourists are seldom flattering and often downright hostile. Sometimes they are worldly men, determined not to be impressed; sometimes, like tourists of every age, they find that reality disappoints their imaginative conceptions; often they are resentful and feel exploited when they find they have to pay—and pay handsomely—to visit a shrine which they feel to be a part of their birthright. And they are often critical of the Dean and Chapter's neglected stewardship. Both Addison in 1710 and Washington Irving in 1835 find a consoling melancholy as they wander about. The vanity of human ambition, now 'crowded together and jostled in the dust,' parsimony 'doling out . . . a little portion of earth to those whom, when alive, kingdoms could not satisfy.' Addison's sense of the diminution of mankind embodied in the building was, nevertheless, not borne out in his own obsequies in 1719, when he lay in state in the Jerusalem Chamber and, ever the presumptuous gate-crasher, contrived a burial among the kings in Henry VII's Chapel. In the persona of Sir Roger de Coverley in *The Spectator* he had been critical of indifferent guardianship: shown the headless figure of Henry V, he expostulated: 'You ought to lock up your Kings better; they will carry off the Body too, if you don't take care.' Oliver

Goldsmith, in 1765, is disgusted. First he has to pay three pence, a national reproach 'so to tax a curiosity which tended to the honour of the English people'. His protest to the gate-keeper is shrugged off by brute economic reality: 'As for that there three-pence, I farm it from one — who rents it from another, — who hires it from a third, — who leases it from the guardians of the temple, and we all must live.' Next he is disappointed by the black coffins, rusty armour, tattered standards, and slovenly figures in wax. A tomb-shewer leads him around, uttering lies, and then dares to ask Goldsmith for money. 'What, more money! still more money! The guardians of the temple . . . should not permit you to squeeze this from every spectator. Shew me the gate', and he

The silver head of Henry V's effigy was stolen in 1546. But at sunrise its modern wooden replacement still glitters.

stomped away in a huff. Mr Hutton made a journey to London from the provinces in 1784, and his preoccupations were entirely earthly. Of the Stone of Scone, he reflected that 'its being hard and cold might very well suit the brawny posteriors of a northern monarch'. Charles Lamb, in 1823, is stirred almost to revolutionary fervour by the mortification of being turned out after the service, 'like a dog, or some pro-fane person, into the common street'. He appeals to his friend Robert Southey, who had been a boy at Westminster, to raise a public clamour 'till the doors of Westminster Abbey be no longer closed against the decent, though low-in-purse, enthusiast, or blameless devotee, who must commit an injury against his family economy' to gain ad-mission. 'In no part of our beloved Abbey now can a person find entrance under the sum of two shillings. The rich and the great will smile at the anticlimax . . . tell the Aristocracy of the country, instruct

1809–22
Henry VII's Chapel restored
July 19th 1821
Coronation of George IV
1827
Edward Blore, *Surveyor*
September 8th 1831
Coronation of William IV
June 28th 1838
Coronation of Victoria
1845
William Buckland, *Dean*
1849
George Gilbert Scott, *Surveyor*
1858
Sunday evening services for the working classes
1864
Arthur Penrhyn Stanley, *Dean*
1870
Burial of Charles Dickens
1878 J .L. Pearson *Surveyor*
1887
Queen Victoria's Golden Jubilee
1901
Death of Queen Victoria

Elegiac view of Westminster with Harvesters by Ackerman, 1810.

Facing page: The vault of Henry VII's Chapel 'where stone is robbed of its weight and density, and suspended aloft as if by magic, and the fretted roof achieved with the wonderful minuteness and airy security of a cobweb.'

Washington Irving

them of what value these insignificant piles of money . . . may be to their humbler brethren. Shame these sellers out of the Temple.' Washington Irving crosses the Atlantic to survey 'this wilderness of tombs', is appalled by the mutilation of the monuments, but consoled by the thrilling thunders of the organ 'in full jubilee', and the Chapel of Henry VII, 'most gorgeous of sepulchres, where stone is robbed of its weight and density, and suspended aloft as if by magic, and the fretted roof achieved with the wonderful minuteness and airy security of a cobweb'.

In the first half of the nineteenth century, England clung on tenaciously to what it knew while enormous pressures of social and economic change built up behind the façade of an aristocratic and landed order. The instinctively reactionary political response to the French Revolution, compounded by military triumphs over the French between 1805 and 1815, was sufficient to retard reform for a generation, even though the familiar social order was dissolving like morning mist. When at last the spirit of reform began to prevail in the 1840s, it was then embraced with such energy and determination that the entire temper of the nation, at home, and in its world role through trade, conquest and empire, was transformed as never before in its history. The story of Westminster Abbey from 1800 to 1900 closely matches the larger model. In the first forty years, there is a high incidence of accident, melodrama, absurdity, incompetence and irreverence, each magnified by contrast with the scenes of attempted magnificence and extravagance which they infiltrate. But it is a long farewell to casual comedy. In the 1840s the old order tangles with the new; out of the confusion grows an entirely new spirit at the Abbey, highly serious, dedicated to compelling and challenging preaching, and reaching out, socially, intellectually, theologically to widen its parish and to admit bracing air to the stuffier preconceptions of an Anglican close. This revolution in its identity and function is partially fuelled by major legislative changes which appeared to diminish its importance: the vesting of Church property in the hands of the Ecclesiastical Commissions, the Public Schools Act which removed Westminster School from Abbey control, and changes in local government which removed the ancient civic responsibilities of Dean and Chapter for Westminster, and turned the increasingly squalid suburb into a city with a Lord Mayor and the power of self-government. Released from such entanglements the Abbey found new life and a new role as a national church offering spiritual leadership. William IV in 1831, and Victoria in 1838 — of extraordinarily different character — mark in themselves a transition from luxurious self-indulgence to solemn duty. Even

The narrow streets of medieval Westminster had to yield to progress. Rowlandson's cartoon on Westminster improvements was drawn in 1808.

The Abbey is a confusing place: Visiting sailors bewildered by the monument to Shakespeare in a caricature *c.*1800.

George IV's coronation in 1821 was noted for its extravagance and ostentation.

modern tabloid newspapers would have found it hard to do justice to the amazing scenes of the 1821 Coronation, and might simply have exploded with excitement in a gush of steam: At a cost of over £238,000, it was immensely extravagant. It was the last coronation to stage a procession from Westminster Hall to the Abbey, and a return procession there for a Coronation Banquet. George IV, having)waited so long for this moment, was not disposed to waste it. A raised wooden walkway was built from Hall to Abbey, the better to display the fashions of the Regency Court. The king himself wore a high feathered hat encrusted with diamonds, with long ringlets hanging down the back of his neck. Although a canopy was carried, he walked in front of it, the better to be seen. But he was upstaged outside the Abbey by the foolish Queen Caroline. In November 1820, a bill to deprive her of her title and rights on the grounds of her alleged adultery with an Italian called Bartolemo Pergami had passed its third reading in the House of Lords, with a majority of nine, but had then been abandoned.

So the queen had no place in George's plan for coronation day. But around 6 o'clock in the morning she appeared in her carriage, and was driven from one door to another in an effort to gain entry to the Abbey. Here was meat and drink to the crowds who had been waiting all the fine summer night. Among them Henry Hill, aged 19, waiting in the Sanctuary, was in the thick of the excitement. 'We had by this time changed our hisses into cries of "Off, off." "Shame, shame." The uproar was now quite stunning. I divide the people into sevenths in order to make my calculations as correct as possible. About four sevenths exerted their lungs to the utmost stretch against

her, yelling and groaning like the Indians of North America when setting up their horrible war-whoop, and, by way of seasoning the dish she had thus compelled herself to swallow, some added cries of "Go away to Pergami", "Be off to Como" etc etc. One other seventh expressed their disapprobation by such expressions as these — "Because she can't enjoy pleasure herself she comes to spoil other people's pleasure, selfish cat," "Damn her, she deserves all she gets" etc etc. Another seventh were her friends but ashamed to cheer as they had asserted she had too much sense to come; they contented themselves with saying — "It's a damn shame to treat a woman so." The remaining seventh exerted themselves in her favour by waving hats and bawling out "Queen, Queen". Though all agreed that each ought to be allowed to express his sentiments without molestation from his neighbours. From this general good humour I must except an old woman who sat before me with a bottle of spirits tied up in a dirty handkerchief. My zeal in yelling, hooting, groaning, and crying "Off, off, shame, shame" drew upon me the anger of this woman who tried to stop my mouth with her hands; then shaking her fist at me she kept calling out "Arn't you ashamed to hoot a poor injured 'ooman; if you were a son of mine I'd give it you, you brute, You don't know the value of a 'ooman". At length . . . with an air of triumph which seemed to say "I have hit it", she exclaimed, "He's hired to hiss the Queen, he's paid 5s. a day by Government."

All the fashions of the Regency Court are heaped upon the preposterous figure of George IV for his coronation procession in 1821.

Caroline, who 'looked uncommonly foolish when recrossing the platform to her carriage', after being refused admission at the North door and Great West Door, returned to her house in South Audley Street. A cheering mob followed her carriage. They then adjourned to the houses of several of the ministers, and, after demolishing a few windows, repaired quietly to take their respective shares in the amusements of the day. But within a month Caroline was dead.

Meanwhile, inside the Abbey, the lavish display of the procession was matched gastronomically. In the Nave aisles agents attended from some of the most considerable confectioners in town. Tables of ices, fruit, wine, sandwiches were to be obtained of good quality and upon reasonable terms. Sir Walter Scott was among the congregation, and wrote a detailed account of the ceremonial for the *Gentleman's Magazine*, but at the end, when the king returned to St Edward's Chapel, the insubstantial pageant faded. During his absence, which lasted about ten minutes, the peeresses departed; the box of the foreign ministers was emptied in a moment; the musicians and principal singers abruptly left the quire: and when the King returned, 'he had empty benches, covered with dirt and litter, on the one hand, and the backs of his courtiers expediting their exits with a "sauve qui peut like rapidity", presented themselves to his view on the other.

This mode of clearing the Abbey certainly was a most unpicturesque arrangement!' And after the banquet, fearing inflamed public demonstration he made an undignified return to his palace through the mean streets, led by Lord de Ros who, as a boy at Westminster School, had had every opportunity of getting to know them. Subsequent troubles in the royal household seem mere ripples in comparison with this Hanoverian squall.

Ten years later, William IV was reluctant to have anything spent on his coronation, partly because of his own parsimony and partly because of the volatile state of the country in the agitation preceding the 1832 Reform Bill. But the unprepossessing king enjoyed much popularity despite, or because of, his long infatuation, as Duke of Clarence, with the actress Mrs Jordan, with whom he lived, as man and wife, and produced a numerous family. Macaulay was present for the four-hour-long ceremonial, and was unimpressed until 'the blaze of splendour' at the moment of crowning. In the midst of it all there was still the regular scene of riot when the medals were thrown about, like a party game intended to break down inhibitions and destroy dignity. The Treasurer of the Household scattered them, 'which set all decorum at defiance, the very judges opposite to us, to the discomposure of their Rams' wigs, shoved and jostled each other to get largesse, which set the House of Commons in a roar, clapping etc. Nothing could have been more ludicrous than the appearance of two of the judges, peers, with their coronets over their Caxons, a bell wether with a crown on would have looked more dignified. It was funnier still when Lord Lyndhurst's fell off, but he has been a good cricketer in his day, for he caught it cleverly, and stuck it on his wig again . . . Such larks seem to come straight from a school playground; boys will be boys, especially when judges and peers of the realm. What Talleyrand, who was present, thought of such larks is not recorded. He was noted lending a very attentive ear to that part of the sermon which praised political freedom and a monarch dear to his people's hearts, but when the bishop began to moralise, he departed. On his way out he observed the orderly behaviour of both the people and of Robert Peel's new police force, whose utility was conspicuous.'

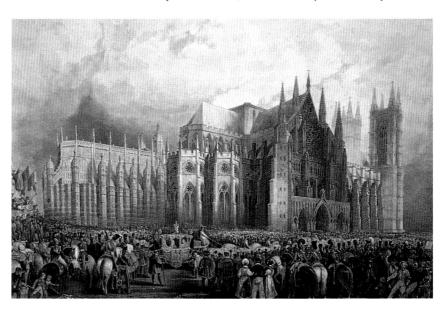

The procession of William IV and Queen Adelaide on its way to the coronation in 1831. Social unrest associated with the Reform Bill and the king's reluctance to spend money made it a comparatively muted event.

The dainty grace of young Queen Victoria, who was 19 when she was crowned in 1838, transcended the many imperfections of the day. The House of Commons broke into a belly-laugh when the aged Lord Rolle missed his footing at the top step when ascending to do homage, and rolled (what else!) all the way down again. They then departed *en masse* before the Communion. There was still the un-dignified scramble for medals behind the throne, much enjoyed by the little pages as they watched the peeresses groping about in all directions. Lord Melbourne's conduct attracted some censure: 'an over-easy cockerhoop (*sic*) manner, so below the occasion, so over at his ease, pushing his coronet to scratch his head close to the Queen whilst bearing the sword of state, that it seemed more like a lot of saucy old vulgar minded hairdressers do and feel, suddenly exalted . . .' The Archbishop of Canterbury and the Bishop of Durham were both clumsy and clueless. The service came to a premature end when the Bishop of Bath and Wells turned over two pages in the service book. 'We ought to have had a rehearsal,' ruefully noted Archbishop Howley in his copy of the service. But the diminutive girl-queen's poise and heart shone through the muddles. Of all monarchs she has left the fullest personal narrative of her coronation day, in her journal. Her consideration, her wide-eyed eagerness, her naïvety mark a new chapter of monarchy:

Sir George Hayter's painting of the coronation of young Queen Victoria in 1838. The Queen wrote a detailed account of the day in her journal.

The geologist William Buckland
became Dean of Westminster
in 1845, and boldly set
about reform.

'My excellent Lord Melbourne who stood very close to me throughout the whole ceremony, was completely overcome (at the Crown being placed on my head), and very much affected; he gave me such a kind, and I may say fatherly look. The shouts, which were very great, the drums, the trumpets, the firing of the guns, all at the same instant, rendered the spectacle most imposing. . . . Poor old Lord Rolle, who is 82, and dreadfully infirm, in attempting to ascend the steps, fell and rolled quite down, but was not the least hurt; when he attempted to re-ascend them I got up and advanced to the end of the steps, in order to prevent another fall. . . . When my good Lord Melbourne knelt down and kissed my hand, he pressed my hand and I grasped his with all my heart, at which he looked up with his eyes filled with tears . . . I repaired to St Edward's Chapel, but which as Lord Melbourne said, was more unlike a chapel than anything he had ever seen; for what was called an altar was covered with sandwiches, bottles of wine etc etc. The Archbishop came in and ought to have delivered the Orb to me, but I had already got it, and he (as usual) was so confused and puzzled and knew nothing, and went away.' Then came the Procession out through the Abbey, and the carriage drive to the Palace. 'The enthusiasm, affection, and loyalty were really touching, and I shall ever remember this day as the Proudest of my life! I came home at a little after six, really not feeling tired.' Fanny Mayow, on leaving the Abbey, had an endearing glimpse of the elderly Duke of Wellington, who had not the patience to wait for his carriage, but gathered all his robes from his pages and said 'run along boys' and off he went, coronet on his head, and being recognised the shout got up and followed him from street to street.

The geologist William Buckland became Dean of Westminster in 1845, and his zeal for reform embroiled him in a prolonged wrestle with Ancient Night. A practical moderniser, he applied a scientific spirit to the condition of the precinct. Gas was laid on, and a fire-engine. Washing facilities were provided for the Westminster

The 13th-century Retable, in the
South Ambulatory, inspired some
of the detail of Sir George Gilbert
Scott's design of the
High Altar (*facing page*).

scholars for the first time in 300 years. He attacked the long constipation of the medieval drainage, and provided the first pipe drainage in London. 'Wash and be clean' was a favourite text for his sermons. At the same time he made the Deanery a place for scientific discussion and experiment, inviting Faraday, for example, to a combined lunch and demonstration of the effects of chloroform administered to 'Beast, Bird, Reptile and Fishes'. But like most reformers, he met much primitive resistance. In digging up the old drains, he released an epidemic of typhoid — *Westminster Fever'* — upon the precinct in May 1848, which was compounded by an outbreak of cholera the following year. He ordered a reform of the food supplied in College Hall, but his good intentions collided with the temper of schoolboys, always a degree or so more reactionary than their masters, who summoned the chef to appear in their midst and then hurled at him the new-fangled treacle puddings Buckland had requested. And he could have made good use of his chloroform upon the Westminster boys in the Cloister Garth, their traditional arena for fighting, in 1846. In the words of Walter Severn, an enthusiastic participant, 'There happened to be a grand consecration of four colonial bishops in the Abbey, so that we were not without solemn music to give éclat to our little entertainment outside. Round succeeded round for more than an hour, when . . . officials from the Abbey [who] had several times tried to put an end to our noisy entertainment, but had water of a very muddy colour thrown over them, and were so roughly used that they had to beat a hasty retreat . . . got one of the masters to enter the Green and stop the fight.' Poor Buckland also had to defend the Abbey against a Chartist mob threatening to overrun it in 1848. It is small wonder that his faculties suffered serious deterioration in the last six years of his decanate, yet it was his spirit, outlook and energy which first set Westminster Abbey on the path of change. He also created a new Choir School, to become the heart of a musical accomplishment unimaginable in the mid-century.

A second powerful force for reform was George Gilbert Scott, appointed to succeed Blore as Surveyor of the Fabric in 1849. Described as 'the first rapist with a timid and careful manner', he set quite new standards in respect for and care of Gothic buildings. The broken grille of Eleanor of Castile's tomb, the battered statuary of Henry V's Chantry, the opulence of his new Reredos Screen behind the High Altar (1866–73), the

The canopy of Scott's screen for the High Altar (1866–73) — practice for St Pancras Station?

Detail from Scott's Screen

The great North Portal, many times reconstructed, but still the image of magnificence appropriate to the royal entrance to the Abbey.

Facing page: The 13th-century Chapter House restored by George Gilbert Scott. It was one of the early meeting-places of the House of Commons.

The Chapter House in 1861, before its rescue by George Gilbert Scott from its function as a Public Record Office.

provision of central heating (1867), his reconstruction of the great North Portal ('Let me earnestly, on my knees if necessary, intercede for this work . . . it will immortalise the Dean and Chapter who undertake it' was an argument dripping with temptation)—his loving recovery of the 13th-century Chapter House from battered Record Office: such was the range of tasks to which he devoted himself with scrupulous integrity. He successfully opposed the proposal to demolish St Margaret's Church to improve the view of the Abbey; he unsuccessfully proposed the building of a 'Campo Santo' opposite the Palace of Westminster to purify the Abbey's Gothic lines by the removal of all monuments inserted after 1647. His dislike of superfluous marble derived from Pugin, Charles Barry's collaborator in the Victorian Gothic rebuilding of the Palace of Westminster after the fire of 1834, who had fulminated against the Abbey's 'incongruous and detestable monuments' with their 'cumbrous groups of pagan divinities'.

The physical reforms of Buckland and Scott were matched in 1858 by a bold reform of the Abbey's ministry, linking the principles on which the Christian church was founded with the new phenomenon of a densely populated industrial working class. Under pressure from the success of popular evangelistic Sunday-morning services, Dean Trench decided to provide a similar service in the Nave. The start was unpropitious: half an hour before the service, timed for 7 p.m., over two thousand people were waiting outside on a freezing December night. When the gate was unlocked, there was a stampede to sit in the chairs specially hired from the Crystal Palace. Policemen patrolled the aisles; there was no heating; the congregation, more accustomed to mission halls, were unable to contribute to the services though later the Abbey had the psalms and hymns printed on calico and hung from the pillars. But the new gaslights provided brilliant lighting as over three thousand people crowded in 'with masses standing anywhere they could. Throughout the sermon you could have heard a pin drop.' Dean Trench preached for forty minutes on the theme of the barren fig tree. At the end he turned directly to the congregation: 'One word in conclusion. Christ gives as a token of his kingdom, that the gospel was preached to the poor. There are some of the poor here tonight—would there were more. Let me say . . . a word to them. Others we cannot hinder coming here; but it was you

An *Illustrated London News* drawing of Sunday-evening service in 1861. Services for the poor had been introduced by Dean Trench in 1858, and attracted people in their thousands. The recent installation of gas-light had made evening services on this scale possible for the first time.

Unlike Henry James, Disraeli was enthralled by the sight of so many people in the Abbey. Disraeli met Dean Stanley in Whitehall on the last Sunday in December, and said he wished to go into the Abbey to hear Canon Farrar preach. His statue stands in 'Statesmen's Aisle' — the North Transept.

we had chiefly in our eyes when these services were designed. You may be meanly clad, but on that account you are all the more welcome to us. . . . . We want the ignorant, the careless, and the profane. . . . . You, the poor, complain sometimes that the rich shut you out from the church. If you would come here in such numbers as to shut them out from the services of the Abbey, we should be all the better pleased'. The walls of privilege audibly tumbled as the Abbey strove, however patronisingly as it may sound to us, to become a one-nation church. In 1876 Disraeli met Dean Stanley in Whitehall on the last Sunday in December, and said he wished to go into the Abbey to hear Canon Farrar preach. The nave was packed, and Prime Minister and Dean had to stand precariously together on the pedestal of a monument. Disraeli was enthralled: 'I would not have missed the sight for anything—the darkness, the lights, the marvellous windows, the vast crowd, the courtesy, the respect, the devotion — and fifty years ago there would not have been fifty persons there!' That Dean Trench's initiative succeeded was not to the liking of the privileged Henry James who in 1877 walked down to Westminster Abbey on Good Friday afternoon, through the parks densely filled with the populace, shuffling elder people and sprawling poor little smutty-faced children. 'When I reached the Abbey I found a dense group of people about the entrance, but I squeezed my way through them and succeeded in reaching the threshold. Beyond this it was impossible to advance, and I may add that it was not desirable. I put my nose into the church and promptly withdrew it. The crowd was terribly compact, and beneath the Gothic arches the odour was not that of incense.' *Esprit de corps*, maybe?

Arthur Penrhyn Stanley was reluctant to succeed Dean Trench in 1864. He did not want to move to 'that church of tombs'. But once installed, he combined the intellectual modernism of Buckland and the populism of Trench in an impetuous and fiercely energetic seventeen-year obsession with Westminster Abbey that made it the pre-eminent church in England for preaching and controversy. He may have owed his appointment to Queen Victoria's devotion to his wife, Lady Augusta Stanley, who as Lady-in-Waiting had been the Queen's chief support at and after the premature death of Prince Albert in 1861. Victoria was always uneasy about Stanley, however — 'so cold — and, to me, as if he were of no sex — though he is so good and clever and writes and preaches so beautifully'. She even disliked his short hair. But he continued to move in the royal circle. The Stanleys held a tea-party in the Deanery in March 1869 for Victoria to meet some of her more distinguished subjects: Browning, Grote, Lyell and Thomas Carlyle, 'a strange-looking eccentric old Scotchman', in the Queen's opinion, 'who holds forth, in a drawling melancholy voice, with a broad Scotch accent, upon Scotland and upon the utter degeneration of everything'. Not an obviously successful social mix, maybe, but the knowledge of royal support bolstered Stanley's confidence. He was no stranger to controversy. His appointment had been attacked from

the Abbey pulpit by the conservative Canon Christopher Wordsworth, who thought Stanley's adherence to the truth of the Bible to be only skin-deep. 'If we hold our peace we shall shake the confidence of the people in the moral courage and honesty of the clergy.' As a Broad Churchman, Stanley tried to transcend theological factions, and, imbued with a missionary spirit, sought out the finest preachers in the land for the Abbey pulpit irrespective of their theological orthodoxy. He initiated, by example and by invitation, a great phase of popular preaching which regularly filled the building to overflowing. His aim was to commend the Abbey to the public, and to every class of that public. He was courageous enough to face down the protests at the communion of a Unitarian in 1870, when over two thousand priests and deacons signed a petition against the acceptance of 'one who openly denies our Lord's eternal Godhead'; in 1871, in the teeth of fierce criticism he sanctioned a performance in the Abbey of Bach's *St Matthew Passion*. He was populist enough to spend most Saturday afternoons taking parties of working men on tours of the Abbey, 'to draw out the marvellous tale that lies imprisoned in those dead stones', as he had declared in his Installation sermon. The marvellous tale was told over again through his tireless researches into the Abbey's history and their published consequence, his *Memorials of Westminster Abbey*, which went through many editions and made the story of the place attractive and widely available. 'That church of tombs' soon acquired a macabre fascination for him as he began to search out and excavate the royal graves. Night after night with a few staff to assist he burrowed away. To Queen Victoria he was known as 'that body snatcher'. The historian J. A. Froude joined him one night. 'It was the weirdest scheme — the flaming torches, the banners waving from the draught of air, and the Dean's keen eager face seen in profile had the very strangest effect. He asked me to return with him the next night, but my nerves had had quite enough of it.' No site was too sacred. Queen Elizabeth's coffin was found to be standing upon and crushing the coffin of her half-sister Mary I; the opening of Richard II's tomb proved the absence of the jawbone stolen by Andrewes a hundred years earlier, and placed the king's skull in the hands of Lord Conway, when 'a hard brown knobby thing like two walnuts united fell out of the skull through the round hole at its base into my hand. It was the shrivelled-up double-lobed brain.' A large pair of plumber's shears was a surprising find in the same tomb. A long hunt for the exact location of James I's coffin ended one day in 1869 when Archbishop Tait was at a meeting in the Jerusalem Chamber. Stanley's excitement at bringing them together was ecstatic: 'Stand back! Stand back! and let the first Scottish Archbishop look upon the first Scottish King of England.' Henry III's tomb was opened, revealing an oak coffin covered with cloth of gold, woven in bands of stars and foils. A party gathered some days later to open the coffin, but an unusual restraint prevailed: the feeling was that there was insufficient historical motive to warrant it. But the vault of the House of Stuart was irresistible. Gaining entry to it from the South Aisle of Henry VII's Chapel, below the tomb of Mary Queen of Scots, Stanley

Queen Victoria, in Cheyneygates, a room in the Abbot's house, now the Deanery.

'That church of tombs.' Lord Chief Justice Mansfield declared he did not want one, but was still treated to one of the largest tombs in the North Transept.

found 'an awful scene': 'A vast pile of leaden coffins rose from the floor, some of full stature, the largest number varying in form from that of the full-grown child to the merest infant, confusedly heaped upon the others, whilst several urns of various shapes were tossed about in irregular positions throughout the vault, in this chaos of royal mortality.' The vault was revisited in 1977, when there were fears of a gas leak. Coffins and their attendant bowel boxes still stood in ranks but by now the coffins were disintegrating. Within that of Charles II could be seen only the sodden, slimy and almost formless remains of the king with the ribcage just discernible.

Spellbound as he was by existing tombs, Stanley was reluctant to consign space to new ones. There were only fifteen funerals in his time, including those of David Livingstone, and, in 1869, Lady Palmerston, when a short-sighted guest fell into the open grave and had to be pulled out. Lady Augusta Stanley, who died in 1876, was buried, by Queen Victoria's command, in Henry VII's Chapel, the Queen herself watching the funeral, in an unprecedented act of royal grief, from the Abbot's Pew, high up at the south-west corner of the Nave. Thomas Carlyle slipped from his place, and ran by the side of the coffin, making strange noises.

In a melodrama entirely fitted to its subject, death, controversy, graves, secrecy and midnight visits wove themselves together around the most notable funeral of Stanley's time, when Charles Dickens died in June 1870, burned out at the age of only 58. The first intention to bury him at Rochester was challenged by a leading article in *The Times* urging Westminster Abbey as the only fitting place. Stanley waited for Dickens's family and friends to respond. At 11 o'clock on Monday June 13th, he had a visit from John Forster, Dickens's friend and future biographer, and Dickens's son, Charles junior. Their meeting launched twenty-four hours of feverish excitement and mystery narrated by Stanley himself in a document written in his own hand. Forster had three conditions to put to the Dean before they could reach agreement. The first two—only two mourning coaches, and no plumes, trappings, or pomp—Stanley accepted as being no concern of his. Then Forster said: 'The third condition is that the place and time of the interment shall be unknown beforehand.' The Dean replied: 'To this condition I am perfectly willing to consent . . . But look at the circumstances: a leading article in *The Times* requesting his burial: the public by this as well as by their own feelings are on the tip-

The clutter of tombs in inconvenient places: an oversize James Watt temporarily parked in St Paul's Chapel. Behind it is the tomb of Lewis Robessart, Lord Bourchier, standard-bearer to Henry V, now *(above right)* restored and repainted.

The earliest known photograph of the West Front taken in the mid-1850s when Victoria Street, a new thoroughfare, was being driven through Westminster's decaying tenements, and when Charles Barry's Houses of Parliament were under construction.

toe of expectation: the remains, now at Rochester will have to be removed to London: is it possible under these circumstances to preserve the secret? It is possible, but only on one condition — that you do not say anything yourselves on the subject, but that this very night you shall bring the body from Rochester, and I, after the public have cleared out of the Abbey, will have the grave dug in Poets' Corner when night has fallen. If you will be here at nine o'clock in the morning before the usual service, the secret may be kept, and the interment shall be performed.' At six o'clock that evening Stanley and the Clerk of the Works chose the spot. At midnight came a thundering knock on the Deanery door. A reporter from the *Daily Telegraph*. 'Dickens's body has been moved from Rochester. Is he to be buried at Westminster? If so, when?' Stanley's servant said that the Dean was asleep and could not be disturbed. Stanley's account continues: 'At nine o'clock in the morning a solitary hearse with two mourning coaches drove into Dean's Yard. It attracted no observation whatever. . . . The coffin entered with the twelve mourners, and was sunk into the grave in presence of these few spectators. It was a beautiful summer morning, and the effect of the almost silent and solitary funeral, in that vast space of the Abbey, of this famous writer, whose interment, had it been known, would have drawn thousands to the Abbey, was very striking.'

As they left, Stanley asked Forster if he would allow the grave to be kept open for the remainder of the day. He said: 'Yes, now my work is over, and you may do what you like.' A flock of reporters arrived, too late, at 11 o'clock. Rumours had spread, and from Tuesday June 14th to Thursday June 16th, when the grave was left open, thousands filed in, 'every class of the community were present, dropping in flowers, verses, and memorials of every kind, and some of them quite poor people, shedding tears.'

Not all were pleased. Rochester had had a grave dug there, and felt cheated; Samuel Butler, maverick Victorian, was contemptuous: 'They have buried Dickens cheek by jowl in the very next grave to Handel. I should not mind, I suppose, but it saddens me that people who can do such things can become Deans of Westminster.'

Quiet days, and congested ones. A solitary horse and cart trundles past Henry VII's Lady Chapel in the 1880s; in 1996 traffic brutalises the place.

Social and political disturbances — by Irish nationalists, rioters and suffragettes — were not uncommon in Abbey services between 1880 and 1914.

Charles Dickens was buried in secret in Poets' Corner in June 1870. Once the funeral was public knowledge, the grave was left open for two days while thousands of Londoners from all social classes crowded in to pay tribute.

A late-Victorian period piece: the family of Dean Bradley poses on the roof of the West Cloister, *c.* 1897.

As a young man quartering London on foot night by night, Dickens's imagination had been captivated by the Abbey. 'Westminster Abbey was fine gloomy society . . . suggesting a wonderful procession of its dead among the dark arches and pillars, each century more amazed by the century following it than by all the centuries going before.' The simple ceremony on that bright June morning was a fit quietus for that restless spirit.

Stanley died in office. After the loss of Lady Augusta in 1876, he seemed to wish to do so. From his deathbed in July 1881, he sent a message to the Queen: 'I am yet humbly trustful that I have sustained before the life of the nation the extraordinary value of the Abbey as a religious, national and liberal institution.' It was a just claim. Under Stanley the Abbey had become the national church. It was the flagship of fine preaching and intellectual ferment. The tradition of popular sermons, lasting about forty-five minutes, established by Stanley and Charles Kingsley was sustained after them by Farrar, Gore and Henson, though the character of the Abbey's theology shifted from Stanley's latitudinarian preference towards Christian Socialism and the Oxford Movement, partly because of Henson's rueful recognition that 'the cultured class has generally ceased to go to church'. Stanley's large vision was brutally put in perspective by an uncultured reluctance to go to church: his own funeral arrangements had to be changed to suit the Prince of Wales's attendance at the first day of the Goodwood race meeting. Stanley had once been tutor to the Prince, and his preference for the gee-gees elicited a memorable rebuke to 'Dearest Bertie', signed 'Your devoted Mama. V.R. and I'. Matthew Arnold, one of the distinguished pall-bearers, in his late poem 'On Westminster Abbey', an elegy for Stanley, grieved for him as a lost child of light, who 'to men's hearts this ancient place endear'd'.

Modern times were encroaching. In 1884, during the agitations about Home Rule for Ireland, the Fenians threatened to blow up the Abbey. In scenes we thought unique to our advanced age, handbags and parcels were checked at the door for sinister substances. Dr Haig Brown was challenged by a constable to open his bag: 'Only my sermon; not half so explosive as Canon Farrar's.' Fears were set aside for the celebration of Queen Victoria's Golden Jubilee in 1887, staged as a re-enactment of her coronation. The clumsy refurbishment of the Coronation Chair aroused the indignation of the *Athenaeum* magazine. It has been 'handed over to some barbarian to be smartened up, and he has daubed it the orthodox Wardour Street brown and varnished it! . . . The throne of six and twenty monarchs has been vulgarised into the semblance of the hall chair of a Cockney Gothic villa.' But the Queen didn't notice, or didn't mind; with her dead husband the first of her thoughts, everything else seemed a little dim or unreal, as if a charade of which she was weary: 'I sat alone (Oh! without my beloved husband, for whom this would have been such a proud day!) where I sat forty-nine years ago . . . my robes were beautifully draped on the chair. The service was very well done and

managed. The Te Deum, by my darling Albert, sounded beautiful, and the anthem, by Dr Bridge, was fine, especially the way in which the National Anthem and dear Albert's chorale were worked in . . . when the service was concluded, each of my sons, sons-in-law, grandsons, and grandsons-in-law, stepped forward, bowed, and in succession kissed my hand, I kissing each; and the same with the daughters, daughters-in-law, granddaughters, and granddaughter-in-law. They curtsied as they came up and I embraced them warmly. It was a very moving moment, and tears were in some of their eyes.' It sounded an interminable family party.

Latitudinarian, Tractarian, Christian Socialist, Evangelical, Unitarian, Oxford Movement, Catholic Emancipation; idealism, controversy, earnestness, fire and fever: the issues that had aroused such passion and energy in Victorian England were beginning to fade. The fervour of theology in its joust with science for primary esteem in the popular imagination was to be insufficient. The burial of Charles Darwin, a non-believer, in the Abbey in 1882 'broke new ground'; the rules had changed. There had to be room in the national church for national figures, irrespective of their theology. Emile Zola, paying a visit in 1893 while a service was in progress, sounds the modern note.

Zola: 'I did not know this was still a Catholic church.' Vizitelly: 'It is Church of England—Protestant.' Zola (astonished): 'Protestant? Well, all that is very much like Mass to me.'

The distinctions over which the Victorians had agonised and battled were fading.

Queen Victoria's Golden Jubilee Service on June 21st 1887, painted by W. E. Lockhart.

Charles Barry's Victoria Tower of the Houses of Parliament, seen from the little Cloister, formerly the Infirmary Cloister.

10.

Our Age

1901 onwards

Major renovation
1973–95

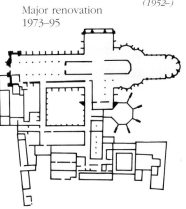

The Abbey workmen, 1904.

A sedan chair originally belonging to Lord John Thynne, Canon and Sub-Dean from 1831 to 1881, was still in use in the Abbey precincts in the present century, though by then it had acquired wheels. The bottom fell out in Dean Robinson's day, when the eager young men who shared the Deanery with him were too vigorous while taking the Dean's sister to a service. Traditions lingered long at Westminster despite the intense pressures for change created by two world wars, the communications revolution and the inexorable drive towards in-stitutional professionalism. Elderly canons and minor canons, fortified by lifelong tenure of their residences, persisted in their autocratic and often eccentric ways as late as 1980. In the 1930's Canon Donaldson would rise early on a Monday in summer to book the College Garden tennis court for the only time in the week allotted to the housemasters of Westminster School. When the moment came he would set up his deck chair in mid-court and snooze on it for the entire two-hour period. In the 1950s Minor Canon Perkins's trousers sometimes had to be diplomatically hidden to deter the very deaf dignitary, a fixture since 1899, from breaking into solemn occasions. He wandered into the Abbey, presumably with trousers on, just as the coffin of Field Marshal Lord Ironside was being carried out after the funeral service. 'Who's he,' bellowed Perkins, 'and where are they taking him now?' Canon Marriott had been known to appear in the Abbey in full regalia but carrying his bowl of breakfast porridge before him. In the 1970's, Canon Adam Fox, aged over ninety, still took long rambles round the city, from which he often had to be escorted home. In the 1980's Christopher Hildyard, a Minor Canon since 1923, shuf-fled arthritically through the Cloisters to early Communion most Sunday mornings. Such figures will be seen no more; the gain in efficiency is offset by the loss of continuity.

Elderly clerics, however venerable, can be hazardous on public occasions. The coronation of Edward VII in 1902, postponed for two months at only twenty-four hours notice because of the king's appendicitis, was jeopardised by an aged and near-blind Archbishop Frederick Temple and the

Dean Armitage Robinson
holding the Abyssinian Cross
outside the Cloisters. The cross
was a gift to the Abbey for the
Coronation of Edward VII
in 1902.

August 9th 1902
Coronation of Edward VII

June 22nd 1911
Coronation of George V
Herbert Ryle, *Dean*

1914–18
First World War

November 11th 1920
Burial of the Unknown Warrior

May 12th 1937
Coronation of George VI

1939–45
Second World War

May 11–12th 1941
Air raid ravages Abbey
and Precinct

November 20th 1947
Wedding of Princess Elizabeth
and Philip Mountbatten.

1950
Theft of the Stone of Scone

June 2nd 1953
Coronation of Elizabeth II

1959
Eric Abbott, *Dean*

1965
Ninth Centenary Year;
'One People'.

1973
Peter Foster, *Surveyor*

1973–95
Exterior stonework restoration

1974
Edward Carpenter, *Dean*

1986
Michael Mayne, *Dean*

1988
Donald Buttress, *Surveyor*

1996 Government returned
Stone of Scone to Scotland

1997
Wesley Carr, *Dean*

1999
John Burton, *Surveyor*

equally aged and unreliable Dean Bradley. Temple had to be lifted from his knees and carried to his chair, and scrolls of large type held in front of him during the service. When Temple turned at the moment of crowning to take the crown from Bradley, he found that the Dean had wandered away with it. On its retrieval, Temple placed it back to front on the king's head. Another fixture was Frederick Bridge, who held the position of Abbey organist for forty-three years, from 1875 to 1918, and had commissioned from Sir Hubert Parry the anthem 'I was glad' for the 1902 coronation. Its success then made it as indispensable a piece of coronation music as Handel's *Zadok the Priest*. Bridge, a bluff and ebullient character, nicknamed 'Westminster Bridge' by Edmund Gosse, was himself a prolific composer of mostly third-rate anthems, which he would often include in the services. It was disconcerting to meet him on the regular walk in St James's Park that Abbey people took between morning service and lunch to be greeted by: 'Did you like the anthem? Lovely thing, wasn't it? I composed it.'

The old order enters the 20th century: Edward VII at the head of his Coronation procession in 1902.

The indignity of being sand-bagged: the tomb of Elizabeth I during the First World War. Despite alarms from bombing and Zeppelins, the Abbey itself was undamaged between 1914 and 1918.

Facing page: 'At the going down of the sun, and in the morning, we will remember them . . .' The Unknown Warrior's Tomb at the West End of the Nave, at sunrise.

The coffin of the Unknown Warrior draped in the Union Jack entering the North Portal on November 11th 1920

A new king had been crowned, a new Dean installed, in the same year of 1911: George V and Dean Ryle. Radical challenges to the settled order they represented soon followed. Militant suffragettes targeted the Abbey in 1913 and 1914. Ryle recorded the disturbance of a service in 1913: 'After the Seventh commandment mænads set up yowling: at first we thought someone had a fit or a seizure, but the howling became more tuneful and in unison. Needless to say, I went on steadily with the Commandments; Alcock worked his organ energetically; the boys shook a bit, but steadied themselves down; the vergers, assisted by the congregation, ejected about a dozen.' On June 11th 1914 a suffragette bomb exploded in St Edward's Chapel, damaging the Coronation Chair, and on August 2nd militant suffragettes interrupted the Archbishop of Canterbury's sermon, 'The Eve of War'. Then came the Great War itself. The Home Front had little idea of how to prepare for the first war involving air attack. In the Abbey the principal monuments were encased in timber frames with sandbag cladding; watchmen, hosepipes, buckets and water tanks were at the ready; one bomb, which failed to explode, was dropped near the Choir School in Dean's Yard; the Norman Undercroft was used by residents for security during air-raids: Sir John Gielgud, then an Honorary Scholar at Westminster School, recalls being shepherded down the Dark Cloister at the threat of Zeppelins. The Abbey was unharmed, but only by good fortune. Dean Ryle reflected at the end of the war that 'we look back upon those nights, and we realise how powerless we were to avert the most terrible catastrophe.' Powerless to ward off disaster he may have been, but his response to the challenge of the war was imaginative and powerful. Beginning with the Anzac service in April 1916, he instituted a series of special services, eighty-six in all before his retirement in 1925, which complemented Stanley's endeavour to make the Abbey a national church. Special services which matched the nation's mood and met the nation's need were, from Ryle's time onwards, habitually associated with the Abbey.

Armistice Day arrived on November 11th 1918, with the official announcement at 11 a.m. 'At 12 noon,' recorded Ryle, 'we held a rapidly extemporized service of thanksgiving attended by everyone in the place and by hundreds who poured in from the street. People streamed in, took their part, kneeling, praying, sobbing—and outside the roar of the shouting and cheering multitudes swept on like a cataract of jubilation.'

But the act of Ryle's that most strongly captured the nation's heart and which in itself changed the popular view of the Abbey more than any other single episode in its story was the burial of the Unknown Warrior on Armistice Day 1920. Credit for the idea belongs to David Railton, an army chaplain, who took it to Ryle, who in turn secured the approval of king and government. A committee chaired by Lord Curzon presided over the plans. On November 7th an unidentified body from each of four battle areas—the Somme, the Aisne, Arras and Ypres—was brought to Brigadier-General Wyatt, who randomly selected one. This body, placed in a coffin of Hampton

Court oak, was conveyed by HMS *Verdun* from Boulogne to Dover, together with six barrels of earth from the Ypres Salient. It was carried by train to Victoria, then by gun-carriage to the Cenotaph in Whitehall, which George V unveiled, then onwards to the Abbey, where it was received by one hundred holders of the Victoria Cross. A short service followed, with Kipling's 'Recessional' and the hymn 'Lead Kindly Light'. At the committal the king scattered battlefield earth from a silver shell, and the padre's flag which Railton had used as altar cloth and shroud on the Western front covered the coffin. It still hangs close by in St George's Chapel. In the next two weeks, one and a half million people filed past the grave in homage, and the image of the Abbey as national church had been renewed. Near the Unknown Warrior, as the fierce century wore on, memorials to Winston Churchill and Louis Mountbatten, men whose lives and deaths similarly united the nation's passions, were placed in grief and gratitude.

But not all eminent remains and reputations were acceptable. Lord Byron, nearly a century dead, was rejected by Ryle since 'a man who outraged the laws of our Divine Lord and whose treatment of women violated Christian principles of purity and honour should not be commemorated in Westminster Abbey'. It took another sixty years before a memorial slab to Byron ('I should prefer a grey Greek stone over me to Westminster Abbey') was at last dedicated in the enlightened decanate of Edward Carpenter. His reasoning doubtless included the reflection that the treatment of women by a substantial proportion of the men already buried or commemorated within might not have withstood too close a scrutiny.

As a Royal Peculiar, the Abbey has long been accustomed to recognise no authority but its own in all matters of policy, provided that the sovereign's displeasure was not incurred. To set their own course in their own way, however idiosyncratic, is one of the many distinctive pleasures of the Dean and Chapter of Westminster. *The Times*, as the voice of public sentiment, had influenced Dean Stanley when Dickens died in 1870, as we saw, but the fitness of the building for the body of the novelist was not in doubt. A dean has only to carry his chapter with him to establish whatever liturgical style he prefers and if the consequence is a stretch of clear water between the Abbey and the Anglican mainstream, or the Abbey and the Archbishop, so much the better. If its 'peculiarity' is not affirmed, it may disappear. So Dean Ryle, though evangelical in temper, encouraged the practice of processions with banners and candles, and the enriching of the vestments by wearing of fine copes on festival days. 'Rather the road to Rome, isn't it?', remarked Randall Davidson, Archbishop of Canterbury, after attending one such service. 'But I like your way of going to Rome.' The Chapter's decisions about the liturgy generally pass

The Union Jack which the army chaplain David Railton had used as an altar cloth on the Western Front covered the coffin of the Unknown Warrior at the burial in 1920. It now hangs, threadbare, in St George's Chapel, near the tomb.

King George VI and Queen Elizabeth (the Queen Mother) with the Bishop of Lichfield (middle) and Canon Elliott (right) with children of the Almonry after the Maundy Service on April 18th 1946.

unchallenged. Congregations, after all, find their own levels. The Authorised Version of the Bible and the Book of Common Prayer are not often heard in principal services in the 1990s; there are a few sad hearts, doubtless, but the worshippers keep coming. From time to time, however, there is a hiccup. This or that scheme suddenly touches a tender nerve, in the establishment, or public opinion generally, and people who seldom, or never worship or visit there suddenly feel possessive and are outraged at what 'they' are proposing to do to 'our' Abbey. Now the Chapter has to dance with wolves. There was a furore in 1928 when Dean Foxley Norris found a donor who was prepared to build a new sacristy between the Abbey and St Margaret's joined to the east side of the North Transept. As soon as the proposal was publicised, there was clamour in the press, and much establishment fur flew as the great and the good opposed one another in battle. A mock-up was put in place in an effort to reassure everyone but the damage had been done, the offer was withdrawn, and the Chapter retreated to reassess its peculiarity. The decisions by the present Chapter to fill the empty niches above the Great West door with statues of 20th-century martyrs, and to commission a memorial to the 'Innocent Victims of War, Oppression and Violence' to parallel that of the Unknown Warrior have polarised opinions in those parts of society which promulgate their opinions. 'Hands off the Abbey' is then a common cry. Yet the Abbey has to be renewed if it is to continue to serve a living purpose. Those who serve it perceive that need more acutely than those who see it as museum, ikon, or branch of Madame Tussaud's, though the imaginative act that commands the nation's approval will always be hard to choose.

Figures of the 20th-century martyrs, including Dietrich Bonhoeffer and Martin Luther King, in preparation at the stonemasons Rattee and Kett. They now stand in the niches above the Great West Door.

Four coronations in fifty-one years were consequences of Victoria's long reign and the premature death of George VI. Predictably the management of these occasions became highly professional, as it had to, given the worldwide attention they attracted as the practice of ceremonial monarchy elsewhere was largely swept away by violent change. The coronations of George V in 1911 and George VI in 1937 were free from disruption and accident. Dean Foxley Norris had a minor scare on coronation morning, May 12th 1937, when the Imperial Crown, which he had to carry into the Abbey, and which he had noted in the Jerusalem Chamber the evening before, was missing. So he had to process empty-handed through Cloisters and Abbey to St Edward's Chapel, where he found that some official busybody had already placed it on the altar.

But the party mood of Coronation Day 1937 was a brief respite. The fragile order of the 1930s was crumbling. When the Second World War was declared, the Abbey's movable treasures were quickly evacuated:

Ten statues of martyrs of the twentieth century fill the niches above the west doors. Below them are figures of Truth, Justice, Mercy and Peace—four of the great virtues for which Christians have laid down their lives.

The Dean, Paul de Labillière, standing in the North Quire with the Sacrarium behind, views damage caused by the air-raid on Westminster on the night of 10–11th May 1941.

the Coronation Chair to Gloucester, effigies and statues first to Boughton House, Northamptonshire, later to Mentmore, the Muniments and most precious books also to Boughton, and then on to an air-conditioned cave in Aberystwyth prepared by the National Library of Wales; the Stone of Scone was buried secretly beneath the Abbey, and a plan for locating it sent to the Canadian Prime Minister. In 1940 and 1941 Westminster was in the front line of war. Sixty thousand sandbags were piled around the fixed monuments of the denuded Abbey. In 1940 there was only minor damage: a bomb in Old Palace Yard peppered Henry VII's Chapel with shrapnel, shattering glass, holing the stonework and dislodging a great pendant; an incendiary bomb passed through the roof of the Jerusalem Chamber without igniting it. Fire-watchers night by night manned observation posts high on the roofs: they were heroically organised by Tom Hebron, and equally heroically fed by Alice Marshall, the source of whose bacon-and-egg breakfasts was one of the war's best-kept secrets. Emergency water tanks were fitted and a control room set up in the Pyx Chapel in the East Cloister. No human preparations, however, could have staved off the devastation of the blitz on Westminster on the night of 10th–11th May 1941. Canon Don, later Dean, was on duty that night and told the story. The sirens sounded at 11 p.m. and the extent of the gunfire indicated a heavy raid. At 11.25 the first incendiaries fell on the South West Tower, but were swiftly extinguished. Then a hail of them glanced off the steep pitch of the main roof without piercing the lead, and landed on the library and the canons' houses in Little Cloister. Many could be extinguished as they came to rest against the stone parapet; one ignited the Triforium roof above the Unknown Warrior, another the east side of the North Transept, but Abbey staff brought both under control. But the Library roof was ablaze, water pressure was too low from ground level, and the storage tank in the South West Tower was emptied in the attempt to extinguish it. Then a second storm of incendiaries set on fire the Deanery, and most of the houses around Little Cloister, and the Abbey's own team lost control of the fire, mainly owing to the shortage of water. Desperate calls went out to the fire brigade, who were themselves in desperation. The promise of 'priority for the Abbey in an emergency', given beforehand to the Dean, could not be honoured. Fire brigade pumps at last arrived at 2 a.m. but precious time was lost by their having to lay a hoseline to the river. By now the Deanery, four houses in Little Cloister, the old monastic dormitory and Burlington's building for the Westminster Scholars were all in conflagration, and an incendiary had lodged inaccessibly in the Lantern Tower above the crossing, which was also blazing. At this moment it seemed that the whole of the Abbey would be engulfed. Molten lead cascaded from the Lantern, bespattering pulpit, lectern and the eastern-most Choir stalls. But then the blazing woodwork crashed to the floor, where the fire brigade and Abbey fire-watchers could contain it. A gaping square of sky peered in upon them. There were no injuries, no high explosive bombs. Much was lost, but more was saved. The 'all-clear' at last sounded at 5.30 a.m. 'The smouldering ruins continued to emit smoke for many hours to come indeed it seemed that the dawn would never break. A thick pall of smoke hung over London and kept the daylight at bay. It was as though the very heavens were conspiring to add to the prevailing gloom.

Reading the Gospel at the Abbey Eucharist on St Peter's Day.

Canon Barry was also on duty as air-raid warden that night. In the course of it he watched helplessly while historic buildings blazed, tried in vain to fight the fire in his own house, saw everything he possessed reduced to ashes, saved the Abbey by a desperate telephone call to high places at 3 am when all other help had failed and communications broken down, and toured his parish of St John's Smith Square visiting the scenes of disaster. At 8 a.m, dressed in sports shirt and sodden flannel trousers he celebrated Communion in the SPG Chapel in Tufton Street, and took the morning service there at 11 a.m. Still scantily clad (it was all he had left) he drove to Reading for a preaching engagement, and went on at nightfall to a relative in Oxford. Next morning, in that unbombed city, he went out to try to buy a few necessities in order to help him start life afresh. On going to one shop to buy a razor he was confronted by a young lady with painted nails behind the counter who, apparently outraged that anyone should suppose the unobtainable obtainable, fixed the scruffy figure with a hostile eye and asked icily, 'Are you aware that there is a war on?'

Princess Elizabeth was married to Lieutenant Philip Mountbatten on November 20th 1947.

There were silver linings. Lawrence Tanner, Keeper of the Muniments, surveyed the desolation with disbelief and horror, but then saw that the monastic buildings had been laid bare, medieval stone walls standing out everywhere in the jumble and that the whole place was alive with antiquarian discoveries. A Service of Christian Witness shortly after the raid marked the start of the Abbey's continuing dedication to the ecumenical movement and pairs of rare black redstarts came to nest and raise families among the ruins.

The war ended, except at 19 and 20 Dean's Yard, where the new Westminster junior school and Canon Smyth failed to find a neighbourly accommodation. The rebuilt precinct changed its look, but not its character. Princess Elizabeth was married to Lieutenant Philip Mountbatten. The Stone of Scone, so cunningly concealed during the war, was retrieved and restored to the Coronation Chair—but not for long. In a sequence of events worthy of the highest traditions of British farce, a group of amateur Scottish Nationalist burglars succeeded in making off with it in December 1950. After a slow drive

The Stone of Scone beneath the seat of the Coronation Chair, built on the orders of Edward I to house it. Seven hundred years after its capture it was returned to Scotland, by government decree, on 30th November 1996. Except for coronations it is now on display at Edinburgh Castle.

The coronation theatre on June 2nd 1953.

south in an unheated car, Ian Hamilton, with a jemmy and other tools, hid behind a statue in the Abbey at closing time. Discovered by a night-watchman, Hamilton pretended he had been locked in, and was released with great kindness at the West door. Further reconnaissance led the group to the builders' yard near the door to Poets' Corner, into which a car could be driven at night. Two nights later, on Christmas Eve, the jemmy easily forced the door, and they were in. The same tool was used on the front of the wooden shelf of the Chair. The four-hundredweight-lump of sandstone came out in a rush, and broke in two pieces on the floor. Now it was easier to move. Hamilton dragged the main chunk through the Abbey on a coat to the waiting car. It was no sooner outside when a policeman appeared. Kay Mathieson, the driver, and Hamilton now pretended to be lovers, and got into a clinch. Pleading that they'd arrived too late to find a hotel, they held hands while the constable offered them consoling cigarettes. Suddenly there was a rumble and thump of the approach of the other piece of the stone. The policeman stiffened. The 'lovers' pretended it was time to leave, and drove away. Hamilton went back to the Abbey on foot, but found no sign of the accomplices or the other part of the stone. Back at the car he discovered that he'd lost the keys. So for the third time that night he entered the Abbey, where he found the keys while crawling about on hands and knees. Driving the car back to the yard, he heaved his capture single-handedly into the back and drove off, meeting the others by chance in a nearby street. They hadn't thought what to do with it. After driving randomly around Southern England, they left it openly in a field. Realising they had not been followed, they retrieved it almost at once, hid it in a wood in Kent, and set off for Scotland, surviving another encounter with the police. Returning two weeks later to collect it, they were appalled to find gypsies encamped on the very spot, but a guarded explanation secured their silence. The Stone was taken home; police investigations made no progress. The publicity coup was complete when, again unchallenged, they placed the Stone on the high altar of the ruined Arbroath Abbey on April 11th 1951, where the forces of law and order bravely recaptured it and returned it to Westminster.

But in July 1996 the government announced its decision to return the Stone to Scotland, except for a coronation. Seven hundred years of guardianship by successive Abbots and Deans of Westminster were thus brought to an end for a doubtful political advantage, and the Stone, which, out of context, is only just another stone, is likely to lose much of its symbolic significance severed from the Chair, Chapel, and Abbey which have conferred upon it a sacramental and constitutional authority since the coronation of Edward II in 1307. In Scotland there was no audible rejoicing at the decision. In 1950, the 'thieves and vulgar vandals' were not prosecuted, though the police felt they had evidence enough to convict. 'Oh yes, it was worth doing', wrote Hamilton, now a distinguished Scottish advocate. It has been less easy to break into the Abbey since, of course.

So the coronation of Queen Elizabeth II on June 2nd 1953, though deluged by the kind of rain specially reserved for English summer festivities, celebrated both the return of the Stone of Scone and the admission, for the first time, of television cameras, though the opposition to them was strong, and the decision in their favour a close call. It was an important decision, for the monarchy as well as the Abbey. Once inside, as both institutions have found, they stay, like inconvenient relatives who come for a weekend and stretch out their legs at your hearth for ten years.

The first half of the 20th century had been, for obvious reasons, an exercise in survival rather than re-newal, with the exception of Ryle's imaginative response to the challenges of the First Great War. The coronation of 1953 can now be seen as a watershed: in the years that followed it, the Abbey has devoted itself to two parallel courses of self-renewal, of its fabric, and of its ministry.

The more visible of these leads us into complex territory. Since the appointment of Sir Christopher Wren in 1698, there have been seventeen Surveyors of the Fabric whose task has been to conserve and repair the building. Few, if any, of these men have been villains and vandals, though there has been no lack of uninformed and ignorant opinion seeking to pillory them. The ground rule is that whatever is done to the Abbey gener-ates opposition. But materials wear out. Stone in a dirty city decays. Wood rots, or is devoured, or is burned. 'Conservation' and 'repair' are frequently incompatible. As the present Surveyor, Donald Buttress, reminds us, 'All great buildings change if they are to remain alive: they live on only through the continued care of each succeeding generation.' The Abbey has been recased many times. It is a surprise to most visitors to learn that the only extensive remaining area of medieval stone on the exterior is the 15th-century work of the west portal, around and above the Great West Door. So each Surveyor has to cross a mine-field. His only possible strategy involves thoroughness (given the costs, there is no argument for short-term patching) and scholarship refined by sensitivity towards the spirit of the building, and its successive creators and preservers.

Three major restorations were directed by Wren and Hawksmoor between 1699 and 1745, James and Benjamin Wyatt between 1809 and 1822 and Blore, Scott and Pearson, successive 19th-century surveyors, between 1827 and 1897.

The fourth major restoration began in 1973, and its completion was celebrated by a thanksgiving service in October 1995. The twenty-two-year programme cost £25,000,000: less than the cost of a single Tornado fighter, as the Dean observed in his address. Funds were all

Elizabeth II crowned on June 2nd 1953.

New glass in the West Window of Henry VII's Chapel commemo-rates the restoration of the entire Abbey between 1973 and 1995.

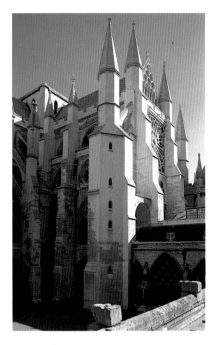

The South Transept restored.

Facing page: Flying buttresses carry the thrust of the roof across the Cloister on the South side of the Abbey.

The organ case.

raised privately through the generosity of individuals and companies from all over the world. A substantial share was raised by the selfless devotion of Tommy Thompson, the Irish 'magician with money', who worked himself to death in the cause. Without him the two most recent Surveyors could have done nothing. The new cross on the western gable is their tribute to him. The preliminaries to the great feast were the cleaning of the interior by Dykes Bower in the 1950s and 1960s which included the washing off of Scott's shellac to restore the pearly-grey lightness of the Caen and Reigate stone, the replacement of damaged Victorian stained glass by glass of greater translucence and the restoration of brilliant colour to many of the early monuments. Then from 1973 to 1988 Peter Foster, a meticulous and methodical Surveyor, began the daunting scheme of external restoration, rendered urgent by the hiatus of two wars and the failure of the stone used in the previous century. Replacing Chilmark stone with Portland, in fifteen years he completed the North and South Sides and Transepts, including the delicate reconstruction of the flying buttresses above the cloister. When Foster retired in 1988, a human flying Buttress, Donald, a northerner with combative energy, independence and directness, discovered the vocation to see the restoration through to the end: first Hawksmoor's West Towers, where rusting iron cramps and rainwater penetration required major surgery, and then Henry VII's Chapel, where the decay of exposed stone compelled the rebuilding of the cupola tops, parapets and pinnacles, and the recarving of three hundred joyous ornamental beasts—dragons, lions, talbots—which swarm over the exterior like children released into a playground. The upper work was done in white Portland stone, the main structure in Bath stone (for matching not patching) which was then given an ochre limewash as a conservation tactic.

When the prospect of raising a further £5,000,000 to complete Henry VII's Chapel caused the financiers on the Westminster Abbey Trust to blench, the combination of Prince Philip's determination, Lord Harris's optimism as chairman of fund-raising and the Surveyor's impassioned cajolery won them round. Buttress, always ready to see off the opposition—to lime washing, to gilding the bosses and shields, to replacement rather than patching of stone and timber—was determined to do 'a proper job'. The rise of the heritage industry may not allow future Surveyors the freedom enjoyed by Buttress and his predecessors, but it has every reason to applaud their collective achievement. Besides, it is rather the judgement of the future, than the present, to which each Surveyor must submit himself.

The second and less visible strand in the story of the Abbey's self-renewal has been its ministry. It has no parish, so in order to fulfil a Christian vocation it has to reach out to those in need, not least to counterbalance the weight of the established order brought to bear upon it on

The Choir in Dean's Yard, at the Choir School fête.

The Chapel of St Benedict, adjoining the south transept, was for many years blocked by a bookstall. Its removal has opened up both the Chapel and its monuments.

national occasions—Royal and Civic events, Remembrance Day, Battle of Britain Sunday, the Judges' service—which could so easily become top-heavy, compelling the Abbey to travel always in a first-class carriage. To have avoided that reductive destiny is largely due to the four Deans and the Chapters they have led since 1959: Eric Abbott, Edward Carpenter, Michael Mayne and Wesley Carr.

There was a long way to go when Edward Carpenter joined an unfriendly Westminster as a young canon in 1951. Life in the precinct was contentious, often irascible and Dean Alan Don was too unworldly and too kind to bring his fissile colleagues into unity. After a Chapter meeting rejected Margaret Hollis's request for a drier for her family's nappies, he approached Mrs Carpenter to ask in all innocence: 'Tell me, Lilian, what is a nappy?' The spirit of accessibility at Westminster began with Eric Abbott, an immaculate figure of great personal magnetism, especially for women, with as wide a circle of friends, correspondents, god-children as any man in London. His background, Principal of Lincoln Theological College, Dean of King's College, London and Warden of Keble College, Oxford, had given him an easy rapport with the young. He was a great listener, both compassionate and discreet, and many individual crises were solved in late night meetings in the Deanery. His was, necessarily, a very personal ministry, but his distance from the everyday life of the precinct had the effect of encouraging the germination of a sense of family among his colleagues. Wives and children began to meet, and to matter. Nappies were no longer unknown.

Towards the middle of Abbott's decanate came the Abbey's Ninth Centenary year, 1965, celebrated under the banner of 'One People'. The stimulus and the striving of a year full of events made it a turning-point in the Abbey's redefinition of its unity and purpose. One people, all faiths; the barriers down. That the late Basil Hume, Catholic Archbishop of Westminster, was invited to preach in the Abbey on the occasion of his enthronement, that the annual Commonwealth Day observance now includes all the major religions of that grouping of nations, that the Dalai Lama was a regular guest at the Deanery in Edward Carpenter's time, and celebrated his 47th birthday there with an English birthday cake, that a jazz band played at the memorial service for Philip Larkin: all were seeds sown in 1965.

Edward Carpenter succeeded Eric Abbott in the Deanery in 1974. Unlike

his predecessor, he had little or no dress sense, and was the despair of those who like their deans properly turned out. He was probably the first truly democratic Dean of Westminster: a good socialist and lover of soccer, who consciously sought to treat everyone, royalty and workmen, alike. He made time for everyone, using the same cheery tone and manner for all. Enthusiasm, directness, *bon-homie* and forgetfulness comprised a distinctive Carpenter style far removed from stuffiness. Royal events were liberated from formality. To celebrate the Queen Mother's 80th birthday, she was invited to an informal evening tour of the Abbey in the company of the Abbey family. Over refreshment in the Jerusalem Chamber, the Dean presented her with so large a commemorative volume that she had to put down her glass to receive it. Carpenter, who was celebrating his own birthday, absent-mindedly picked it up and finished it while she was saying a few words. When she turned for her glass it was gone. There stood the benign guilty Dean. 'You've taken my drink!' came the comic accusation, and the stiffness of the occasion was dissolved.

The apparently inexorable increase in the pace of city life, the press of engagements, rising numbers both of visitors and staff, anxieties about security, and about publicity, were already making the Abbey a less easy place to hold together and to direct. Michael Mayne succeeded Carpenter in 1986. He and the Chapter have not only seen to completion the task of restoration, but have also paid the most scrupulous and stylish attention to the content and presentation of services, as befits a dean who was for seven years head of religious programmes for BBC radio. The use of the Revised English Bible and the Alternative Service Book, and the introduction of a lantern altar on the same level as, and visible by, the congregation have been liturgical changes with a popular emphasis. The Eucharist has been established as the central act of worship on a Sunday in place of traditional Matins, incorporating in both as high a degree of participation as the building and form of service admit, and, for the first time since the Reformation, the wearing of Eucharistic vestments. And the Abbey has pursued a broad ministry to the wider community, especially to those affected by HIV and AIDS, and to the homeless and those who provide for them. The inert procession of huddled blankets each night along the shop fronts of windswept Victoria Street brings both afflictions to the Abbey's own doorstep. It seems appropriate that prominent among those whom the Abbey has chosen to commemorate in Mayne's time are the socially or sexually marginalised figures of Oscar Wilde, John Clare, A.E. Housman, and the innocent civilians slain by 20th century history.

So here it stands, this 'close-packed chaos of beautiful things and worthless vulgar things', after more than a thousand years of tumultuous history. It has somehow resisted the despoiling of two religious revolutions, fire, neglect, vandalism, riots, air-raids, Westminster schoolboys, 18th-century funerals, tomb rifling, tourists, sea-coal, industrial pollution, traffic. Simply contemplating its miraculous survival nurtures faith. But what is it for, and who is it for? How successful is it, and what of its future? I put these questions to many

A window commemorating A. E. Housman in Poets' Corner is fitted into place on September 17th 1996.

The painted roof of the Lantern was designed by Stephen Dykes Bower as part of the programme of post-war restoration at Westminster.

Facing page: St Faith's Chapel, beyond the South Transept, is for quiet prayer.

This timeless figure heating tar for the roofs brings thoughts of hell-fire into the heart of the Cloisters.

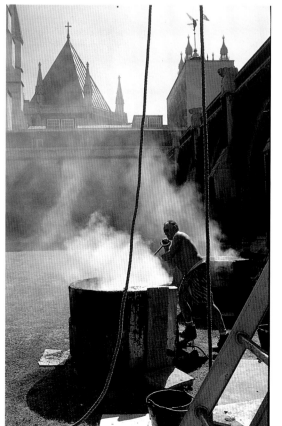

people who have been associated with the Abbey in our time, for when a historian reaches the present his material becomes largely guess-work, and to offer an accurate likeness of contemporary attitudes is his best hope.

The Abbey's purpose is Christian witness. The forms of this witness are always changing; the heart remains the same. Chiefly such witness is expressed in services. The very core of its being is to present at its best the Anglican tradition in words and music. The stabilising rhythms of Matins at 7.30, Eucharist at 8.00, and Evensong at 5.00, day in and day out, echoing the monastic order, frame and contain the intervening frenzy of the working day. This foundation of routine is a vital counterpoint to the turbulence of a busy city, the floods of visitors, the special and experimental services and the concerts. For those who know the Abbey well the most intense memories are of services, often the great services, when the Abbey has to embody and release a national mood, and is subject to intense public scrutiny: the funeral of Lord Mountbatten, the memorial services for Laurence Olivier, Bobby Moore, Les Dawson, Peggy Ashcroft, or services of celebration, when congregations break into spontaneous applause, as when the late Cardinal Hume, installed as Roman Catholic Archbishop of Westminster, preached at Evensong, and the Benedictine monks of Ampleforth returned to sing Vespers for the first time since the Reformation; or as when a renewed South Africa returned to the Commonwealth with tears of joy. The same grapple of feelings also marks the highly charged Children of Courage service held each year. But equally treasured are the small-scale services in a secluded corner: a christening on a winter afternoon in Henry VII's Chapel, commemorations around a tomb or memorial—Tennyson, Dickens, Dr Busby—attended by a handful but witnessed by the whole place, 'Little Commem', when the scholars of Westminster School sing plainsong Compline by candlelight in Henry VII's Chapel and lay roses on the tomb of Elizabeth I every November 17th, the date of her accession to the throne.

Yes, the Abbey is for services, and few ever see or appreciate the efforts, liturgical, musical, administrative, that underlie the quality of the finished product. But who is it for, this finely tuned enterprise? The Abbey has no parish. There are barely a hundred regular worshippers, a few of them gentle oddballs who have adopted the place, or have wanted it to adopt them, liking the anonymity of a church without the narcissism of parochial business. But there is an Abbey Community: dean, canons and their families, the 150 full-time employees on the pay-roll, choristers, ex-choristers, honorary stewards, vergers, Abbey Assistants, almsmen, members of Westminster School, rooted in the precincts for about 800 years. Many of these may not worship in the Abbey often, but it is still their nurse;

they feel that they belong, and in times of need they are supported. Though the leisured days of the 1930s, and their Abbey cricket team and Concert Party are gone; and though the almost leisured 1960s and 1970s have vanished, together with the weekly informal 'drop-in' for wine at the Deanery or one of the canon's houses, the community nourished by the place is still strongly affirmed at Christmas, Easter, St Peter's tide, Foundation Day and at times of either greeting or farewell to those who serve the Collegiate Church of St Peter. Yet the Abbey has no choice about wearing the habit of hierarchy alternately with that of community. It is also a marker for the British establishment, where social structure is tenacious, which looks to it from time to time to embody its view of the world. The Abbey is like an actor pushed into a theatre in the round to give a non-stop performance to a capacity audience. He scarcely knows which way to face and what expression to wear. It is hard under such pressures also to acknowledge the efforts of the backstage crew.

It is especially hard to know how to face the tidal waves of up to three million visitors a year, the vast majority of whom do not attend a service and are not practising Christians. The tension between the Abbey as a tourist honey-pot and the Abbey as a living place of Christian witness is not easily resolved, despite the efforts made to link them. Icons in the Nave where visitors may light candles invite a simple, universal gesture of reverence, and a daily service there at 12.30 hushes departing tourists into tip-toe curiosity. During Evensong each day in the Quire, the Nave is freely accessible for visitors to sit, if they are reluctant to commit themselves wholly to the service. The music flows westwards, and the choir, men and boys, brilliantly scarlet and white against the muted grey stone, can be watched processing in and out. Something rare, however unintelligible to many visitors, is regularly going on.

The balance sheet for this daily invasion is inescapable. The Abbey receives no funding from the Church of England, the Crown or Parliament. It has to generate all its own income. Visitors contribute 80 per cent of the turnover, which pays everyone, clergy and lay staff, and maintains the building, remedying the attrition of 20,000 hands, lungs and feet a day. The Abbey cannot survive without the visitors who threaten to wear it out. In

such conditions, the diminished quality of everyone's experience, the wear and tear upon the fabric, the throng too numerous and restless for either a sense of holiness or the possibility of education, it was tempting to conclude that, like tourist sites the world over, it was being visited to death by 'the tribes of Adidas, Nike and Reebok' as Alan Bennett christened them in his documentary on the Abbey. Many simply came to meet friends, or to wait for Eurostar. The Nave was bedlam, with jostling crowds and yelling guides. Only one visitor in three went to the east end of the Abbey to see the royal tombs and monuments. The Abbey was out of control.

The Dean (Wesley Carr, who succeeded Michael Mayne in 1997) and Chapter drew up a new strategy. If the Abbey was rescued from frenzy, visitors might again sense the reverence the place deserves, and remember their visits with affection. The plan was called 'Recovering the Calm'. And it succeeded. The key decision was to charge every sightseeing tourist an entry fee to the building. The number of visitors was reduced—though not by much—but the quality of their experience transformed. Instead of pouring out of coaches and hot-footing it into the Nave, they are first calmed by a walk through Dean's Yard to the Cloisters, where they stand in neat, obedient lines like children about to re-enter school from the playground. The preliminaries for individual visitors are psychologically shrewd. Payment is made in a low, dark vestibule—there is no longer the clink of the money changers within the temple—and visitors are given a high quality ticket and brochure bearing the gilded image of Edward the Confessor from the Litlyngton Missal. Great expectations are aroused, and triumphantly fulfilled, when visitors emerge from a cavern into the space, light and height of the transepts. From here people move around reverentially, in whispers; the flow is controllable; marshals with walkie-talkies 'pulse' through groups, each with an experienced guide, and limited in number. Many visitors are calmed further by the handsets they carry, like blessed one-way mobile phones, as intent as if they are listening to God direct. The Confessor's Shrine remains, appropriately, a mystery apart, unvisited, but glimpsed between other royal tombs; the Coronation Chair glows in an unearthly old gold light, raised high at the foot of the 'Scala Caeli', the staircase to heaven leading to and from the Lady Chapel in the east. The Cloisters, through which all visitors must pass, have been cleared of their

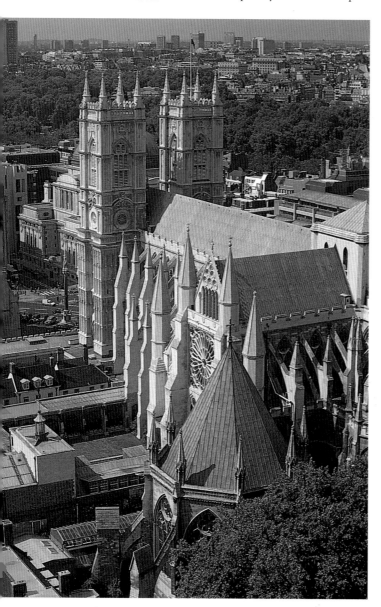

The West end of the Abbey from the Victoria Tower of the Palace of Westminster.

brass-rubbing claustrophobia. Like the interior, where chairs have been cleared away, there is space to stroll, and stand, and look, and wonder. The Nave is largely silent for prayer or reflection. And no one has to pay to pray: the Pilgrim Door on the north side offers free access to those who seek the peace of God.

So the Abbey tries to give all its visitors a genuine welcome, and mostly succeeds. They are not tourists invading, but pilgrims searching for—who knows what? The Abbey has to be for them all, this diversity of faiths and denominations, and those of no faith. It has to offer a friendly welcome to the world, his wife and their children in the hope of making some impression, it hardly matters what: musical, architectural, historical, a smile, an explanation, courtesy. So there are marshals and Abbey Assistants, whose loyalty and love for the place tend to make a vocation of service softened by generous tolerance prevail in what must be one of the most taxing jobs in London. This humane reception committee has learned to deal gently with the marginal people whom the Abbey attracts—addicts, beggars, confidence tricksters, thieves, drunkards, some with flick knives and broken bottles—with the indignant protesting at the entry fee, with the ignorant who ask 'Where are Hansel and Gretel buried?' (an easy confusion between the Babes in the Wood and Princes in the Tower), with the desperate genuinely in need of guidance, with the confused who ask 'Is this Victoria Station?' With patience, interest and talk it is possible to establish rapport with a few, so that visitors can say and feel, when in London once in five years, that 'it's good to be back'. To offer a welcome, to present worship that is not exclusive, to hope that something, not necessarily Christian, or even religious, gets through to some, are neither mean nor cynical objectives. In a bad year there might be three letters of complaint about the discourtesy of Abbey staff. It tries to be a place of tolerance and magnanimity. A rare exception was Biggles, the Abbey cat, half tabby, half tiger, who was in the habit of savaging tourists in the Cloisters. He was banished to the country, but guilty compensation was paid to his forceful personality when he was immortalised in a carved caricature in stone not far from that of the Duke of Edinburgh on the outside of the North-West Tower.

The Abbey has also chosen to bear witness in stone to the chaos and terror of a century nearing its end, in which the building itself came so close to destruction. At the foot of the North-West Tower stands a memorial, simple as a covered well, to Innocent Victims of Oppression, Violence and War. Dedicated by the Queen in 1996, it is the counterpart of the military tomb of the Unknown Warrior nearby, within the West Porch. Ten niches above the West Portal, empty since the sixteenth century, have been at last filled by ten twentieth century martyrs for their faith, killed by their own people, a worldwide spectrum which includes Dietrich Bonhoeffer and Martin Luther King. The most daunting and comprehensive of all challenges in stone, the cleaning and restoration of the exterior of the whole building, and the raising of the £25 million to pay for it, was completed in 1997. Building and carving in stone is itself an act of

Stone caricature of Biggles, the Abbey cat on the North-West Tower.

Outside the west front of the Abbey, a simple circular memorial commemorates the Innocent Victims of Oppression, Violence and War.

faith which links past, present and future. It was a courageous Dean and Chapter to select an inscription which will long outlive them carved in bold lettering to the left of the West Door: 'May God grant to the Living Grace, To the Departed Rest, To the Church and the World Peace and Concord, and To Us Sinners Eternal Life'. Such interweaving of past, present and future with an unflinching look at the world's needs and an affirmation of hope is unlikely to cause embarrassment to successors.

Not by its own choosing, the Abbey was buffetted by storms of publicity in 1997 and 1998. The funeral service for Diana, Princess of Wales, in September 1997, seen by millions across the world, received the kind of accolade every politician must fear as the prelude to opprobrium. So too at Westminster, where its very success seemed to goad the fickleness of public opinion. Through a nightmare peopled by the press, the Abbey was seldom out of the news, beset by critics who, as has always been the way with the National Church, all knew much better than the Dean and Chapter. Through a tense time of provocative public scrutiny, the Abbey conducted itself with commendable patience and dignity. In their decisions, commitments and witness, recent Deans and Chapters have not lacked courage.

And what of the future? What are the Abbey's needs as it enters the new millennium? 'Lavatories' is the common cry. Nothing has changed since Pepys was taken short at the Coronation in 1661, and the question most often and urgently asked is 'Where are they?' Visitors have to be directed across the road to the public lavatories in front of the Conference Centre, where they are more likely to be mown down than to find relief. So the Abbey also needs liberation from traffic, which is a monstrosity. No other city in Europe would suffer it to roar and shudder round the foul asphalt tracks only feet from Henry VII's Chapel, between Abbey and Palace of Westminster, and turning the arena in front of the West Towers, where so many walking routes converge, into a miserable rat-run cum shooting-gallery for human beings who wish to stroll and marvel. It needs better educational provision, especially for parties of visiting children, who tend to arrive ill-prepared and drift round disengaged. It needs a woman canon, say most of the women, and some of the men. It needs free bungee-jumping from the West towers, say the choristers. But the most serious and central challenge is the evolution of its relations with the State. British society is now diffuse, in race, religion,

Below and facing page: The funeral of Diana, Princess of Wales, was written and conducted within six days. 31 million people in the UK as well as billions around the world watched on television.

morality. The Abbey is both peculiarly British and international. Its links with the Commonwealth are marked annually by a highly celebratory Commonwealth Observance, and in the course of the year for each Commonwealth country on its national day.

The Abbey's ancient links with the Crown and through St Margaret's with Parliament will have to take account of cultural pluralism. It is difficult to see how the next coronation, for example, could simply reaffirm the close bond of monarch and Church of England that previous coronations could innocently endorse. To be all things to all men without sacrificing the heart of its Anglican history and Christian identity is a hard road to follow.

But it can be done. The place is alive, and will find a way. This marvellous building, still enfolding all that it has known, has a vast tolerance and capaciousness. It has acquired the power to calm fretfulness, to absorb floods of visitors, oddities of behaviour, local tensions and scandals, to deflect evil, to arouse an extraordinary quality of devotion in those who serve it, of reassurance in those who visit or worship regularly, of welcome to the thousands who step inside once only. By a paradox, the place makes you feel both great and small at once as it first catches you up into its long processional order, and then dismisses you from it. And as the last visitors ebb away and the lights are put out and the doors are sealed and the noise of the city fades, there, coming and going, are the souls of those who also have a share in Westminster Abbey: the three black-robed monks gliding into the Nave at 2 a.m. to rebuke a benighted electrician whose snores were disturbing their Matins; the restless Bradshaw striding up and down the Triforium on the anniversary of Charles I's execution; the mysterious reflective figure standing and gazing down into the Unknown Warrior's grave the night before the burial. The Abbey is for them too. Like a great ocean liner built on Thorney Island but never launched, in each age it gathers souls and harbours them, and bears them silently on not through space, but through time. For ever. For ever? Or may be 'The time must come when its gilded vaults, which now spring so loftily, shall lie in rubbish beneath the feet; when, instead of the sound of melody and praise the wind shall whistle through the broken arches and the owl hoot from the shattered tower; when the garish sunbeam shall break into these gloomy mansions of death, and the ivy twine round the fallen column; and the fox-glove hang its blossoms about the nameless urn, as if in mockery of the dead.'

Bibliography

Sources for this book are too numerous to list comprehensively. The bibliography below includes only the titles that provided extensive material. Reading was done almost entirely in the Westminster Abbey Library and Muniment Room, with supplementary work in the Lambeth Palace Library and the Library of the Literary and Philosophical Society of Newcastle upon Tyne.

Barlow, F., *Edward the Confessor*, Eyre & Spottiswoode 1970
Besant, W., *Westminster*, Chatto & Windus 1897
Bevan, B., *Royal Westminster Abbey*, Hall 1976
Bond, F., *Westminster Abbey*, Henry Frowde 1909
Brooke, C. N., *London: The Shaping of a City*
Carpenter, E. F. (ed.), *A House of Kings*, John Baker 1966
Colvin, H. M. (ed.), *History of The King's Works*, HMSO 1963
Harvey, B., *Living and Dying in England 1110–1540*, Oxford 1993
Jones, W., *Crowns and Coronations*, Chatto & Windus 1898
Lethaby, W. R., *Westminster Abbey and The King's Craftsmen*, Duckworth 1906
Murray Smith, E. T., *The Roll-Call of Westminster Abbey*, Smith, Elder & Co. 1903

Murray Smith, E. T., *Westminster Abbey: Its Story and Associations*, Cassell 1906
Perkins, J., *Westminster Abbey*, Duckworth 1937
Ridgway, J., *The Gem of Thorney Island*, Bell & Daldy 1860
Rosser, G., *Medieval Westminster*, Oxford 1989
Russell, A. L. N., *Westminster Abbey*, Chatto & Windus 1934
Stanley, A. P., *Historical Memorials of Westminster Abbey*, John Murray 1886
Storr, V. E. and J. Perkins, (eds.), *Historic Occasions in Westminster Abbey*, Sheffington 1933
Sullivan, D., *The Westminster Corridor*, Historical Publications 1994
Tanner, L. E., *The Story of Westminster Abbey*, Tuck 1932
Tanner, L. E., *Recollections of a Westminster Antiquary*, John Baker 1969
Walcott, M. E. C., *Westminster*, Joseph Masters 1849
Westlake, H. F., *The Story of Westminster Abbey*, Philip Allan 1924
Westlake, H. F., *Westminster Abbey: The Last Days of the Monastery*, Philip Allan 1921
Westlake, H. F., *Westminster Abbey*, Philip Allan 1923

General Index

Bold numbers = illustrations

Index to Objects

(See next page for Plan) Numbers thus: [C9–10] refers to position on Plan. **Bold** numbers refer to illustrations. Other numbers refer to text.

Continued on p.160

Tour of the Abbey

Including objects referred to in the book.

See *Index to Objects,* pages 157 and 160

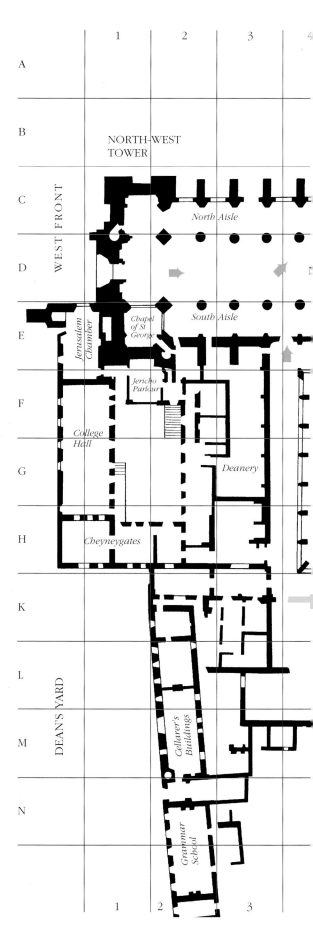

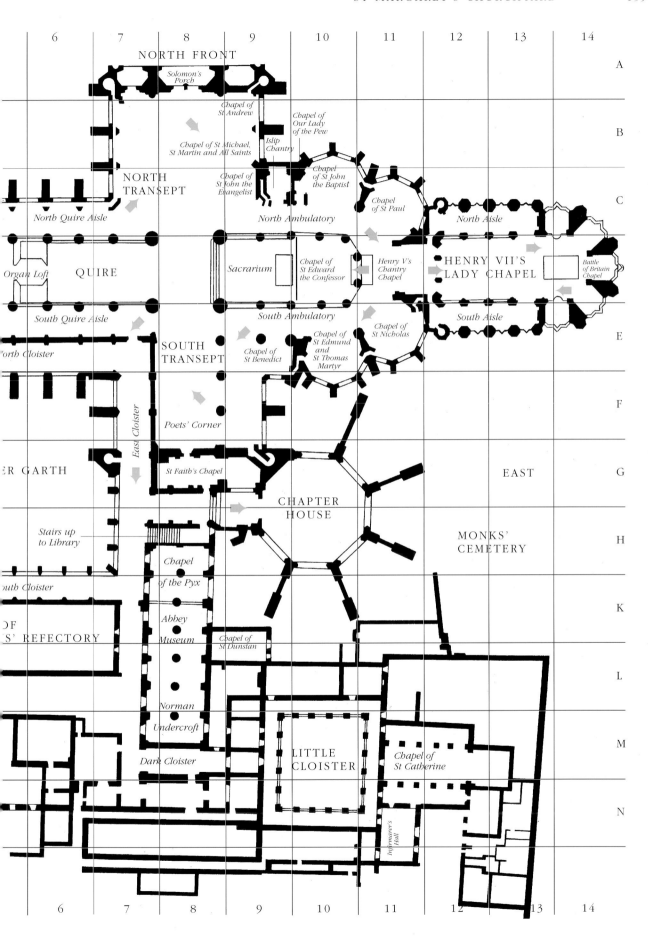

NORTH FRONT

Solomon's Porch

Chapel of St Andrew

Chapel of Our Lady of the Pew

Chapel of St Michael, St Martin and All Saints

Islip Chantry

Chapel of St John the Evangelist

Chapel of St John the Baptist

NORTH TRANSEPT

North Quire Aisle

North Ambulatory

Chapel of St Paul

North Aisle

Organ Loft

QUIRE

Sacrarium

Chapel of St Edward the Confessor

Henry V's Chantry Chapel

HENRY VII'S LADY CHAPEL

Battle of Britain Chapel

South Quire Aisle

South Ambulatory

South Aisle

North Cloister

SOUTH TRANSEPT

Chapel of St Benedict

Chapel of St Edmund and St Thomas Martyr

Chapel of St Nicholas

East Cloister

Poets' Corner

ER GARTH

St Faith's Chapel

EAST

CHAPTER HOUSE

Stairs up to Library

MONKS' CEMETERY

Chapel of the Pyx

South Cloister

Abbey Museum

Chapel of St Dunstan

OF S' REFECTORY

Norman Undercroft

LITTLE CLOISTER

Chapel of St Catherine

Dark Cloister

Infirmarer's Hall

SOUTH

COLLEGE GARDENS

Index to Objects

(Continued from page 157)

Numbers thus: [C9–10] refers to position on Plan. **Bold** numbers refer to illustrations. Other numbers refer to text.

Kings and Queens